Exploring your Further Education Teacher Identity

Offering a new approach for further education (FE) and vocational educators, this practical guide provides the tools and techniques necessary to trace and map professional identities and consider how these evolve and recognise continuing professional development needs.

Exploring the theoretical grounding and key tools in the form of Likert scales and networks of enterprises, this practical guide is packed full of useful tips and case studies that illustrate the practical applications of the tools and the benefits of using them. With key examples drawn from FE and vocational teachers working across the sector, this book is designed to provide insight and CPD guidance for anyone grappling with two or more professional identities. In a changing professional landscape where teachers are expected to fulfil multiple roles simultaneously, this book has the power to reshape how teachers reflect on their dual or multifaceted identities.

Exploring your Further Education Teacher Identity is essential reading for vocational FE teachers and their managers, trainee teachers, and teacher educators who want to better understand their professional identities and feel more in control of where they position themselves.

Abbie Cairns is an artist-teacher working in and researching adult community learning in the UK. She is engaged in both art and teaching practices and splits her time between art practice, art teaching and initial teacher education, and research.

Exploring your Further Education Teacher Identity
A CPD Toolkit

Abbie Cairns

LONDON AND NEW YORK

Designed cover image: © Abbie Cairns

First published 2026
by Routledge
4 Park Square, Milton Park, Abingdon, Oxon OX14 4RN

and by Routledge
605 Third Avenue, New York, NY 10158

Routledge is an imprint of the Taylor & Francis Group, an informa business

© 2026 Abbie Cairns

The right of Abbie Cairns to be identified as author of this work has been asserted in accordance with sections 77 and 78 of the Copyright, Designs and Patents Act 1988.

All rights reserved. No part of this book may be reprinted or reproduced or utilised in any form or by any electronic, mechanical, or other means, now known or hereafter invented, including photocopying and recording, or in any information storage or retrieval system, without permission in writing from the publishers.

Trademark notice: Product or corporate names may be trademarks or registered trademarks, and are used only for identification and explanation without intent to infringe.

British Library Cataloguing-in-Publication Data
A catalogue record for this book is available from the British Library

Library of Congress Cataloging-in-Publication Data
Names: Willis, Larkin, author. | Carver-Thomas, Desiree, author. | Darling-Hammond, Linda, 1951- author.
Title: District leadership for racial equity : lessons from schools systems that are closing the gap / Larkin Willis, Desiree Carver-Thomas, Linda Darling-Hammond.
Description: New York, NY : Routledge, 2025. | Includes bibliographical references and index. | Identifiers: LCCN 2024062255 (print) | LCCN 2024062256 (ebook) | ISBN 9781032938905 (hbk) | ISBN 9781032938882 (pbk) | ISBN 9781003568087 (ebk)
Subjects: LCSH: Educational equalization–United States–Case studies. | Educational change–United States–Case studies. | Discrimination in education–United States–Case studies. | Racism in education–United States–Case studies.
Classification: LCC LC213.2 .W586 2025 (print) | LCC LC213.2 (ebook) | DDC 379.2/60973–dc23/eng/20250507
LC record available at https://lccn.loc.gov/2024062255
LC ebook record available at https://lccn.loc.gov/2024062256

ISBN: 978-1-032-80633-4 (hbk)
ISBN: 978-1-032-80367-8 (pbk)
ISBN: 978-1-003-49781-3 (ebk)

DOI: 10.4324/9781003497813

Typeset in Helvetica
by codeMantra

I dedicate this book to my family: to my mum, who reads every draft; my dad, who built the desk I write at; my sister, who keeps persuading me to take up extreme sports; my nephew, who provides playful distractions; and my grandparents, who proudly tell everyone they meet what I'm up to.

In memory of Roy Cairns (5th January 1937–14th February 2024).

Contents

Lists of Figures	ix
List of Tables	xi
About the Author	xii
Acknowledgements	xiii
Participant Pen Profiles	xiv
Foreword	xvii
Introduction	**1**

SECTION 1:
NETWORK OF ENTERPRISES INTRODUCTION — 11

1. **Multifaceted identities** — 15
2. **What is a network of enterprises and why is it important?** — 30
3. **How to use a network of enterprises** — 44
4. **From use to insight: FE teacher and trainers' reflections on the network of enterprises** — 64

Conclusion — 79

**SECTION 2:
LIKERT SCALES FOR DUAL IDENTITIES INTRODUCTION** 81

5. **Dual identities** 85

6. **What is the Likert Scale for Dual Identities and why is it important?** 100

7. **How to use Likert Scales for Dual Identities** 112

8. **From use to insight: FE teacher and trainers' reflections on Likert Scales for Dual Identities** 130

    Conclusion 142

    Conclusion 144

    Index 147

Figures

1.1	My FE teacher assemblage as a rhizomatic map.	18
1.2	My degrees of community participation (Wenger et al., 2002).	23
2.1	My network of enterprises in the style of Daichendt (Cairns, 2023).	35
2.2	My Wallace and Gruber linear network of enterprise (Wallace and Gruber, 1989).	37
2.3	My monthly network of enterprises example (Cairns, 2023).	40
3.1	My enterprise audit example.	46
3.2	My enterprise mapping example.	47
3.3	My enterprise timeline example.	48
3.4	My network of enterprises three-year block example.	49
3.5	My yearly network of enterprise example.	50
3.6	My monthly network of enterprise example.	50
3.7	My time and passion lens network of enterprise examples.	52
3.8	My time lens network of enterprise example.	52
3.9	My remuneration lens network of enterprises example.	53
3.10	My passion lens network of enterprises example.	53
3.11	My personal lens network of enterprises example.	54
3.12	My professional lens network of enterprises example.	54
3.13	Network of enterprises three-tiered key.	55
3.14	My network of enterprises three-tiered example.	56
3.15	Network of enterprises five-tiered key.	57
3.16	My future planning network of enterprises example.	58
3.17	My goal setting network of enterprises example.	59
3.18	My revisiting network of enterprises example.	60
3.19	My completed network of enterprises example.	62
4.1	Kerry's network of enterprises.	77

FIGURES

6.1	Reproduction of the Artist-Teacher Likert Scale in black and white (Cairns, 2023b).	102
6.2	Artist-teachers' current and ideal identities.	105
6.3	An example of a Likert Scale for Dual Identities.	109
7.1	My yearly Likert Scale for Dual Identities example.	121
7.2	My six-monthly Likert Scale for Dual Identities example.	121
7.3	My monthly Likert Scale for Dual Identities example.	122
7.4	My weekly Likert Scale for Dual Identities example.	122
7.5	My daily Likert Scale for Dual Identities example.	123
7.6	My as-and-when Likert Scale for Dual Identities example.	123
7.7	My current and ideal identity Likert Scale for Dual Identities example, from the 'me' position.	124
7.8	My current and ideal identity Likert Scale for Dual Identities example, from the 'learner' position.	124
7.9	My Likert Scale for Dual Identities visual analysis example.	126
7.10	My Likert Scale for Dual Identities numerical analysis example.	127
8.1	Ronnie's Likert Scale for Dual Identities.	141

Tables

5.1	Dual identity table	86
5.2	Overcoming identity conflict table	94
7.1	My charting experiences example	113
7.2	My recall qualifications and courses example	114
7.3	Likert Scale for Dual Identities five-point scale example	115
7.4	Likert Scale for Dual Identities seven-point scale example	116

About the Author

Dr Abbie Cairns is an artist-teacher-researcher who has a portfolio career that includes teaching in adult community learning (ACL) in the UK. Her research tackles teacher identity, and she is deeply committed to raising the profile of further education (FE) teachers and the sector. Her work aims to improve the lives of those in the role by helping individuals to better understand their identities and how to navigate and transform them.

Abbie has worked in the FE sector since 2017 and has worked in adult education since 2018. She writes and delivers accredited and non-accredited art and digital marketing courses. She is a practising and exhibiting artist who has shown her work nationally. She is a member of the National Society for Education in Art and Design (NSEAD) and sits on the board of Colchester Art Society (CAS). She works with SPACE to facilitate peer feedback and networking sessions for emerging and re-emerging artists in the Essex area.

You can find out more about Abbie's work on her website and social media channels.

Website: https://drabbiecairns.com/home

Instagram: @DrAbbieCairns

Acknowledgements

I would like to show appreciation for the FE teachers and trainers who have contributed to this book, listed below, and the many others who opted for anonymity, without whom the publication would not have been possible.

Audrey Fairgrieve – Beth Curtis – Dr Gary Husband – Elizabeth Draper – Heather Booth-Martin – Jason Boucher – Joyce I-Hui Chen – Kerry E Heathcote – Ronnie Houselander-Cook – Sue Chillingworth – Toby Doncaster. You will learn more about these FE teachers and trainers in their pen profiles presented shortly.

I also extend my gratitude to Bill Esmond, who graciously authored the foreword for this book. Your thoughtful words and insights set the perfect tone for this book and all that follows. Your expertise and generosity have added great value, and I am truly honoured to have your voice as part of this work.

Participant Pen Profiles

Heather Booth-Martin originally trained and worked in the hospitality industry before becoming a teacher in FE. She taught business and hospitality for many years before transitioning into teacher education. She has combined teaching and research, recently completing an EdD, and she now works as a teacher educator in both FE and HE.

Jason Boucher is a professional educator and coach who is articulate, knowledgeable, and people-centred. He advocates for student agency, social justice, and the educational empowerment of all. A firm believer in the power of education to change lives, he is open-minded, non-judgemental, and a lifelong learner. Jason enjoys his own educational journey and is empathetic to others as they navigate theirs.

Dr Joyce I-Hui Chen has been working in different educational sectors for more than 20 years abroad and in the UK. She is Quality Enhancement Manager at a further education college, managing initial teacher education programmes as a centre manager and involved in professional development, organisational development, and quality improvement.

Sue Chillingworth's passion for photography began as a child when her next-door neighbour gifted her a small compact camera for Christmas. Since then, she has learned to see the world through the lens of her camera, developing a love for both the technical and creative challenges the medium provides. She now combines stock photography and teaching with her own creative work.

PARTICIPANT PEN PROFILES

Beth Curtis is a drama teacher and teacher educator who has been working in further education since 2008. She is also a teacher-researcher with a particular interest in the use of creative methodologies. Her doctoral research employed playwriting as a method of enquiry to explore student and teacher experiences of assessment in A Level drama.

Toby Doncaster is an FE English tutor, Edtech enthusiast, and performance coach. He is fascinated by behaviour management tips, resource development, and effective learning strategies. He is passionate about developing strategies to help busy teachers plan and thrive in today's hectic teaching environment.

Elizabeth Draper is Deputy Chair of the English Association, a fellow, a trustee, and a member of the OCR English consortium. Elizabeth has dedicated over 30 years to teaching, including HOD (SFC) and Director of English (FE), Elizabeth as a teacher-activist and a change-maker forges communities of educators in interdisciplinary connecting ways to develop 'Englishes' for meaningful work within and beyond current curriculum.

Audrey Fairgrieve has worked in the FE sector since 1993 and is currently part of the Adult Learning Faculty at an FE college. She is responsible for quality assurance of the provision and supports staff development. She teaches a range of subjects, including languages, digital skills, cookery, and crochet, and she previously held responsibility for teacher training.

Kerry E. Heathcote is a senior leader in the further education sector, a chartered psychologist, and an associate fellow of the British Psychological Society. With experience in custodial, educational, and community settings, she is also a homelessness campaigner and active volunteer. Her PhD focuses on the effective intersectional and predictive use of routinely collected data to support and inform learner outcomes, aiming to improve social justice through a critical realist lens.

Ronnie Houselander is an artist, researcher, and teacher based in Southwest England. Her multidisciplinary practice explores the professional identities of further education practitioners through an arts-based approach. In addition to her research, she works as a creative producer, collaborating with and supporting other artists in developing their projects.

Dr Gary Husband's background is in social care settings, engineering, and teaching and research in further and higher education. He has held several teaching and leadership roles in both the further and higher education sectors in Scotland, England, and Wales. His research interests are focused on the development of the further, adult, and vocational education sectors and engagement with professional and community learning. He leads on the development of educational research at the University of Sunderland and manages the master's provision in Education Studies. He is also a keen amateur musician and archaeologist.

Foreword by Bill Esmond

This book contributes to debates about further education (FE) and the education of adults from several welcome directions. In a world where education and especially vocational studies have been constructed in terms of 'learning,' it draws our attention back to questions of teaching, which are essential to educational practice. It takes a stand on the well-trodden (and too often over-simplified) territory of 'dual professionalism,' a phrase rolled out by successive policymakers, not always for the most commendable of reasons. It also draws attention to arts-based practices, an essential component of further education and indeed of humanity, that the re-framing of education by recent governments as the technicist transaction of commodities (including FE as 'technical education') seems designed to expunge. It introduces the work of an author already capturing attention in this field to a wider audience.

This is a book of possibilities. It draws the attention of teachers to the possibilities for constructing an educational practice that can make a difference in the lives of their students. Its methods are designed to support the struggles of new teachers to create a meaningful identity. But it remains attentive to the difficulties new teachers face. As Abbie Cairns observes early in this book, teachers are often faced with low status, low pay, insecure contracts, and uncertain working hours. Material difficulties and the practical pressures of new roles combine with the unease and anxiety that most new teachers encounter in moving into this very public role, where their every utterance and movement can be subject to question. In environments driven by a relentless economic logic, tutors themselves may not always be able to bring about improvements, leading to further frustrations (James and Wahlberg, 2007). The performative pressures on FE teachers can appear almost designed to drive teachers out of the profession (Colley et al., 2007).

Against this background, this volume draws on notions of dual and indeed multifaceted professionalism as a way of making sense of teachers' lives and identities. This concept deserves careful attention, as all too often this is presented in simplistic terms, as combining occupational expertise drawn from the teachers' past with the performative requirements of teaching. This may provide new teachers with a source of meaning and identity, as their knowledge of current occupational practice may be more up to date than that of established mentors, whose role is often presented in terms of subject expertise rather than guidance about educational practice or pedagogy (Esmond and Wood, 2017). However, the way these relationships are sometimes framed may become a barrier to deeper thinking about how to combine this expertise with understandings of what is entailed in developing a coherent educator identity (Lawy and Tedder, 2011).

Such thinking is little encouraged by recent attempts to reduce FE to the business of providing businesses with skilful and compliant employees. The rediscovery of 'technical education' as a title for the FE sector indicates a willingness to narrow its scope still further. This title refers not only to the layering of an extravagantly funded Potemkin of upmarket-branded qualifications in front of a cash-starved FE sector but hints at a low regard for broader educational and cultural practices, as a recent study of enrichment in colleges discovered (Esmond et al., 2024). For new teachers, especially those in the part-time or temporary roles that have long been essential to the FE sector's functioning, matters of curriculum and qualification may not seem the most immediate of concerns, yet they shape every teacher's practice.

For these reasons, the role of the arts as a source of professional knowledge and of identity has an importance far beyond most accounts of occupational expertise. The arts provide us not only with models of sophisticated practice but with forms of subject expertise that cannot be confined to the procedural. They also provide a key to a cultural sphere beyond the everyday experience of young people and adults alike. In this, they not only complement the educational practice of artist-teachers and others in similar relationships to teaching but can enable the enrichment of curriculum in every subject, providing understandings of the cultural dimensions even of technical subjects, alongside the societal, environmental, and ethical considerations that are too often forgotten.

I hope that readers will enjoy the activities in this book and find them useful in making sense of their role as teachers. This is an occupation like no other, in terms of both its potential to change the thinking of others, if not always their lives, and the incessant demands that its complex relationships open up. Hopefully, this book will also enable them to think about the broader context within which educational practice takes place, discussed in its early chapters and in the notes above. In this spirit, I congratulate the author of this book and wish its readers well in using it as well as in their educational journeys beyond it.

REFERENCES

Colley, H., James, D., and Diment, K. (2007) 'Unbecoming teachers: Towards a more dynamic notion of professional participation', *Journal of Education Policy*, 22(2), pp. 173–193. doi: 10.1080/02680930601158927.

Esmond, B., Kaur, B., and Atkins, L. (2024) 'Beyond subjects and skills or crossing the divide? From additionality to complementarity in college enrichment', *Journal of Curriculum Studies,* pp. 1–17. doi: 10.1080/00220272.2024.2425629.

Esmond, B., and Wood, H. (2017) 'More morphostasis than morphogenesis? The 'dual professionalism' of English Further Education workshop tutors', *Journal of Vocational Education & Training,* 69(2), pp. 229–245. doi: 10.1080/13636820.2017.1309568.

James, D., and Wahlberg, M. (2007) 'The limits of tutor intervention: Understanding improvement in a cultural view of FE learning and teaching', *Educational Review,* 59(4), pp. 469–482. doi: 10.1080/00131910701619357.

Lawy, R., and Tedder, M. (2011) 'Beyond compliance: Teacher education practice in a performative framework', *Research Papers in Education*, 27(3), pp. 303–318. doi: 10.1080/02671522.2010.535615.

Introduction

> **VIGNETTE: ACCIDENTAL**
>
> Lots of things in my professional life seem to happen accidentally. This book is one of them. Teaching was another. With a new university centre heavily advertised on the radio, in the space of a few short hours, I found myself filling out a form and transitioning from art graduate to trainee teacher and I have never looked back.
>
> Cairns, A. (2024) Accidental. Unpublished vignette.

This book focuses on the dual and multifaceted identities of vocational and technical teachers and trainers in further education (FE) in a UK context. Within the pages of this book, I present two identity tools designed for handling these complex identities: networks of enterprises and Likert Scales for Dual Identities. These two tools offer a new approach for FE teachers and trainers to trace and map their professional identities. This book provides you with opportunities to reflect on your current and ideal professional identities and how these evolve. This book helps you explore the various identities you possess, including your vocational and teacher identities, and other past and present roles, such as that of a student. This book makes a significant contribution to our understanding and visualisation of vocational and technical FE teachers' and trainers' identities, and it has the power to reshape how teachers and trainers reflect on their dual or multifaceted identities.

The network of enterprises is a type of diagram first used by American psychologists Doris Wallace and Howard Gruber with creative people at work

(Wallace and Gruber, 1989). This tool can be used to help individuals track numerous enterprises over time, with a focus on continuing towards goals in different areas. This book represents and updates the tool for contemporary use by vocational and technical FE teachers and trainers. I developed the second tool, the Likert Scale for Dual Identities in 2024 as an updated version of the Artist-Teacher Likert Scale (ATLS). The ATLS was a tool that I used in my early research with artist-teachers working in ACL (Cairns, 2023). This tool ranged from one to ten numerically, transitioning from artist to teacher conceptually and red to blue visually. The Likert Scale for Dual Identities tool draws on James Daichendt's (2009) notion that dual teacher identity exists on a continuum.

The network of enterprises and ATLS began as tools for creatives. However, I think they are just as useful for any vocational or technical FE teacher or trainer. The following published literature has shined a light on dual and multi-faceted teacher and trainer identity and how it impacts teachers of all subjects, including, but not limited to, science teachers, art, drama, and English teachers (Rushton, 2021); geography teachers (Brooks, 2016); language teachers (Kong, 2018); and music teachers (Bucura, 2022).

At points in this book, you will be prompted to stop and *Try This!* These activities have been designed to help you consider your dual or multifaceted professional identity. The first activity can be found at the end of the introduction and comprises a handy diagnostic quiz to help you pick the right tool for you, the network of enterprises, or the Likert Scale for Dual Identities, based on your current professional identity.

AUDIENCE OF EXPLORING YOUR FE TEACHER IDENTITY

The intended audience of this book is self-identifying vocational and technical FE teachers and trainers in the UK. Within this sector, we often take up our roles in teaching or training after being practising professionals, whether as artists, like me, or as mechanics, chefs, or hairdressers. This book will also be of interest to you if you are a manager of vocational and technical FE teachers and trainers, a trainee teacher, teacher educators, and vocational and technical undergraduate and postgraduate students. As a reader, it is expected that you will have a background in a vocational or technical area and have transitioned into or plan to transition into teaching in FE. If you are a teacher educator or a vocational and technical lecturer reading this book, the content provided here will be useful for inclusion in professional development modules where exploring professional identity would be beneficial.

FURTHER EDUCATION

FE in the UK can be understood as a diverse and wide-ranging sector that spans several providers including colleges, adult community education providers, local authority providers, third-sector providers, independent training providers, prison education, and employer providers (ETF, 2020). Our work in FE makes a meaningful difference in the lives of those from disadvantaged backgrounds including those from low-income backgrounds and those from marginalised groups (Smith and Duckworth, 2022). As FE teachers and trainers, we are concerned with real people (Duckworth and Smith, 2018) and helping them gain confidence and grow (Gleeson et al., 2015), by offering our learners transformative experiences which enrich their lives (Smith and Duckworth, 2022). Overlooked, our sector is often referred to as the Cinderella sector (Petrie, 2015), however, with the good that the sector does, it might be more appropriate to position ourselves as fairy godmothers, there to offer everyone a second chance (Hafez, 2015).

Within FE, we are held accountable by the Education and Training Foundation (ETF) professional standards for teachers and trainers (ETF, 2022). Despite this we are often faced with low status (Briggs, 2007) and low pay (Augar Review, 2019). The FE sector is also rife with issues around stability, and you may have found yourself with insecure contracts and uncertain working hours (Westminster Hall, 2021). Further, we have become deprofessionalised with the removal of requirements for FE teachers and trainers to acquire qualifications or engage in continuing professional development (CPD) activities (Augar Review, 2019). Instead, we are left with a culture that is focused on mandatory training, which may have left you feeling deprofessionalised (Hafez, 2017). You may have also found that the responsibilities of finding, paying for, and engaging in subject-specific CPD are placed on you (Cordingley et al., 2019).

Working in FE you may have noticed the sector and your role as a teacher or trainer being undervalued (Westminster Hall, 2021) and you will be aware of those working in FE being excluded from the 2024 teachers' pay rise which significantly widened the gap in pay between schoolteachers and FE teachers and trainers (National Education Union, 2024). It may then be unsurprising to you that our sector faces a retention crisis, in part due to pay and in part due to work-related stresses (Petrie, 2015). In 2021, it was reported that over 40 per cent of our colleagues planned to leave the sector and that year on year, there is an increase in the number of FE teachers and trainers leaving their posts after just one academic year (DfE, 2021).

The FE sector is constantly evolving, and those of us working in the sector must adjust to ever-changing expectations, new policies, and work towards meeting Ofsted requirements. Changes in funding, curriculum requirements, and accountability measures can place significant pressures on FE teachers and trainers, affecting our roles and identities. Due to these changes and the challenges that come with them, as FE teachers and trainers we must build resilience in our professional identities (Cordingley et al., 2019). Faced with heavy workloads (TES, 2022), high expectations (Ofsted, 2019), and accountability pressures (Smith and Duckworth, 2022), as an FE teacher you will benefit from understanding your professional identities and your involvement in each identity you embody. It is also my hope that you will benefit from having space to question your professional identity and how you might want to change it. The practical tools provided, the network of enterprises and Likert Scale for Dual Identities, allow you to reflect on who you are and who you want to be professionally.

PURPOSE OF EXPLORING YOUR FE TEACHER IDENTITY

The purpose of this book is to help you, and other vocational and technical FE teachers and trainers navigate your professional identities in an ever-evolving landscape. As a practical guide, this book will remain pertinent for FE teachers and trainers as long as we continue to operate in a world where we must have dual and/or multifaceted professional identities. These tools will only become more important as we continue to diversify our professional identities to fit into a changing landscape. Therefore, the focus of this book is to equip you with the skill sets to juggle dual or multifaceted identities. Without these skills you may find your professional identities in conflict, torn between your vocational and/or technical and teacher and/or trainer commitments.

Additionally, the practical tools provided may have a positive impact on FE teacher and trainer retention and positive impact on teacher and trainer well-being. This is timely, as the Teacher Wellbeing Index showed that teachers wellbeing continues to decline after COVID-19 (Education Support, 2023). Overall, the purpose of this book is to provide you with practical ways of negotiating dual or multifaceted identities.

AIM OF EXPLORING YOUR FE TEACHER IDENTITY

The primary aim of this book is to assist you in reflecting on your dual or multifaceted professional identities and your involvement in each and to allow you to question if you want or need to change these in any way. I have written this book as a practical guide, providing you with theoretical knowledge about dual and multifaceted professional identity and practical knowledge, including step-by-step instructions on how to engage and get the most out of the network of enterprises and the Likert Scales for Dual Identities. As you work your way through this book there will be moments for reflection, questions to answer, and *Try This!* activities to complete. To get the most out of this book I highly recommend engaging in these. I have also included reflections from FE teachers and trainers at the end of each section to illustrate the application of the tools and the benefits of using them to those in the field.

STRUCTURE OF EXPLORING YOUR FE TEACHER IDENTITY

I have written this book in two sections, Section 1 outlines networks of enterprises and Section 2 outlines Likert Scales for Dual Identities. Each section includes four chapters outlined below.

SECTION 1: NETWORKS OF ENTERPRISES

Chapter 1: *Multifaceted identities* outlines the concept of having a multifaceted professional identity in a world where teachers are expected to assume various roles beyond just teaching and vocational expertise.

Chapter 2: *What is a network of enterprises and why is it important?* draws inspiration from the work of Doris Wallace and Howard Gruber, along with their tool, the network of enterprises. The network of enterprises is presented as a tool for tracking and charting identities over time, originally used with creative people at work, and this book expands its use across all vocational and technical FE teachers and trainers.

Chapter 3: *How to use a network of enterprises* suggests updates to the original work of Wallace and Gruber to modernise its use and better capture the fluidity of teacher identity.

Chapter 4: *From use to insight* shares the reflections of FE teachers and trainers on the network of enterprises. The shared experiences are intended to help you better understand and negotiate your use of the tool and the techniques used within it.

SECTION 2: LIKERT SCALES FOR DUAL IDENTITIES

Chapter 5: *Dual identities* begins with a brief outline of the concept of dual identity and dual professionalism in the context of FE. The chapter then introduces Likert Scales as a practical tool for navigating dual identity and presents three case studies from across the vocational and technical FE teacher and trainer landscape.

Chapter 6: *What is the Likert Scale for Dual Identities and why is it important?* refers to the work of Alan Thornton and James Daichendt. The chapter frames dual identities as continuums, with the dual vocationalist-teacher identity situated in the middle of teacher or trainer identity and vocational or technical identity.

Chapter 7: *How to use Likert Scales for Dual Identities* suggests changes to the Artist-Teacher Likert Scale to make the tool accessible to any dual vocational and technical FE teacher and trainer identity, to better capture the of flux of dual identity.

Chapter 8: *From use to insight* shares the reflections of FE teachers and trainers on Likert Scales for Dual Identities. The shared experiences are intended to help you better understand and negotiate your use of the tool and the techniques used within it.

The conclusion reaffirms the significance of comprehending and managing one's professional identity as an FE teacher or trainer and summarises the advantages of utilising the two practical tools presented. The conclusion ends a with short recaps on each tool.

OVER TO YOU

You can engage in this book in one of two ways, the first option is to read it cover-to-cover and the second option is to use the quick diagnostic quiz below to help decide which tool might be most beneficial for you currently. It is worth nothing that you might find it beneficial to engage in both tools across your professional career.

> ### *TRY THIS!* DIAGNOSTIC QUIZ
>
> Use this short diagnostic quiz to assess which tool you might find more beneficial to engage in currently, the networks of enterprises or Likert Scale for Dual Identities. Once you've answered the five questions below, tally up your answers and see which tool aligns more closely with your current preferences and needs.

What is your primary goal in using the tool?

a. To track and manage multiple enterprises over time.
b. To assess and understand your dual identities as a vocationalist and a teacher.

What kind of visual representation do you prefer?

a. A diagram that shows the trade-offs between different enterprises.
b. A scale that represents identity as a continuum.

How important is it for you to have a numerical scale?

a. Not important.
b. Important.

How comfortable are you with the concept of dual identities?

a. Not comfortable.
b. Comfortable.

How much flexibility do you need in the tool?

a. A lot of flexibility.
b. Limited flexibility.

Now, tally up your answers! If you answered mostly "a," then the networks of enterprises might be a better fit for you. If you answered mostly "b," then the Likert Scale for Dual Identities might be a better fit.

REFERENCES

Augar Review (2019) *Independent panel report to the review of post-18 education and funding May 2019.* Available at: https://assets.publishing.service.gov.uk/government/uploads/system/uploads/attachment_data/file/805127/Review_of_post_18_education_and_funding.pdf. (Accessed 23 February 2021).

Briggs, A. R. J. (2007) 'Exploring professional identities: Middle leadership in further education colleges', *School Leadership and Management*, 27(5). pp. 471–485. doi: 10.1080/13632430701606152.

Brooks, C. (2016) *Teacher subject identity in professional practice: Teaching with a professional compass.* New York: Routledge.

Bucura, E. (2022) *Music teacher identities: Places, people, and practices of the professional self.* Münster: Waxmann Verlag GmbH.

Cairns, A. (2023) *Interrogating artist-teacher identity: Transformation in adult community learning.* Doctoral thesis, Norwich University of the Arts.

Cordingley, C., Crisp, B., Johns, P., Perry, T., Campbell, C., Bell, M., and Bradbury, M. (2019) 'Constructing teachers' professional identity', *Education International*. Available at: https://www.ei-ie.org/en/item/25683: constructing-teachers-professional-identities. (Accessed 15 October 2024).

Daichendt, G. J. (2009) 'George Wallis: The original artist-teacher', *Teaching Artist Journal*, 7(4), pp. 219–226. doi: 10.1080/15411790903158670.

Department for Education (DfE) (2021) *Further education college workforce analysis*. Available at: https://assets.publishing.service.gov.uk/government/uploads/system/uploads/attachment_data/file/950958/FE_college_workforce_analysis.pdf. (Accessed 13 September 2024).

Duckworth, V., and Smith, R. (2018) 'Breaking the triple lock: Further education and transformative teaching and learning', *Education and Training*, 60(6), pp. 529–543. doi: 10.1108/ET-05-2018-0111.

Education and Training Foundation (ETF) (2020) *A guide to the further education sector in England*. Available at: https://www.et-foundation.co.uk/wp-content/uploads/2020/08/200729-ETF-FE-Sector-Guide-RGB-v10.pdf (Accessed 13 September 2024).

Education and Training Foundation (ETF) (2022) *Professional standards for teachers and trainers in the further education and training sector*. Available at: https://www.et-foundation.co.uk/wp-content/uploads/2022/04/PS-for-Teachers_Summary-of-Standards_A4-Poster_Final.pdf#:~:text=Professional%20Standards%20Education%20and%20Training%20Foundation%20%20,aspirations%20of%20learners%20through%20your%20enthusiasm%20and%20knowledge. (Accessed 8 July 2022).

Education Support (2023) *Teacher wellbeing index 2023*. Available at: https://www.educationsupport.org.uk (Accessed 15 October 2024).

Gleeson, D., Hughes, J., O'Leary, M., and Smith, R. (2015) 'The state of professional practice and policy in the English further education system: A view from below', *Research in Post-Compulsory Education*, 20(1), pp. 78–95. doi: 10.1080/13596748.2015.993877.

Hafez, R. (2015) Beyond the Metaphor: Time to take over the castle. in Daley, Orr, and Petrie (ed.) *Further Education and the Twelve Dancing Princesses*. UCL IOE Press, pp. 157–164.

Hafez, R. (2017) 'Chapter 18: Inside the Trojan horse: Educating teachers for leadership' in Daley, M., Orr, K., and Petrie, J. (eds.) *The principle: Power and professionalism in FE*. London, pp. 171–176.

Kong, M. (2018) *The hopes and experiences of bilingual teachers of English: Investments, expectations and identity*. Abingdon: Taylor & Francis.

National Education Union (2024) *Pay in further education*. Available at: https://neu.org.uk/advice/member-groups/further-education-teachers/pay (Accessed 13 September 2024).

Ofsted (2019) *Educational inspection framework*. Available at: https://www.gov.uk/government/publications/education-inspection-framework. (Accessed 21 December 2020).

Petrie, J. (2015) 'Introduction: How Grimm is FE?', in Daley, M., Orr, K., and Petrie, J. (eds) *Further education and the twelve dancing princesses*. London: UCL IOE Press, pp. 1–11.

Rushton, E. A. C. (2021) *Science education and teacher professional development: Combining learning with research*. Cham, Switzerland: Springer International Publishing.

Smith, R., and Duckworth, V. (2022) *Transformative teaching and learning in further education: Pedagogies of hope and social justice*. Bristol: Bristol University Press.

TES (2022) *More than 2 in 3 art teachers 'considering leaving' profession.* Available at: https://www.tes.com/magazine/news/general/more-2-3-art-teachers-considering-leaving-profession. (Accessed 21 March 2023).

Wallace, D. B., and Gruber, H. E. (1989) *Creative people at work: Twelve cognitive case studies.* New York: Oxford University Press.

Westminster Hall (2021) *Westminster Hall debate: Third report of the education committee, A plan for an adult skills and lifelong learning revolution, HC 278.* 15 April 2021, 1.30pm. Available at: https://parliamentlive.tv/event/index/f3d210ee-0aab-4050-9fe5-e8b09e5f4ed2. (Accessed 15 April 2021).

SECTION 1

Network of enterprises introduction

Section 1: Network of enterprises introduction

> **Vignette: Who am I now?**
>
> I've been an artist in the studio and a teacher in a classroom – and online. I've been a researcher with books and a student with debt. I've been an artist-teacher and a teacher of skills. I've been a researcher of identity and student for years.
>
> Cairns, A. (2024) Who am I now? Unpublished vignette.

This section outlines the concept of having a multifaceted professional identity, in a world where FE teachers and trainers are expected to assume various roles beyond teacher and vocational expertise. This section draws inspiration from the work of Doris Wallace and Howard Gruber (1989) and their tool, the network of enterprises. The network of enterprises is presented as a tool for tracking and charting identities over time and was originally used with creative people at work (1989). Within this section, the network of enterprises is updated for contemporary use for vocational and technical FE teachers and trainers.

This section is broken down into four chapters: Chapter 1 focuses on multifaceted identities and how these are made up of a complex mix of diverse enterprises that come together to build a sense of self. Chapter 2 looks at what the network of enterprises is and why it is important to those with multifaceted identities. In this chapter, the tool is outlined as being concerned with charting and tracking an individuals' multiple enterprises over time as a means of providing a comprehensive overview of their engagement and goal achievement in each (Gruber and Wallace, 1999). Chapter 2 goes on to suggest updates to the original work of Wallace and Gruber (1989) to modernise the network of enterprises and better capture the fluidity of vocational and technical FE teacher and trainer identity. Chapter 3 outlines how to use the network of enterprise effectively and comprises a step-by-step guide for using the tool. Steps outlined include naming your enterprises, picking a timeframe, assessing the significance of your involvement in enterprises, and future planning. This chapter ends with the opportunity to *Try This!* and create your own network of enterprises. Chapter 4 shares reflections from FE teachers and trainers and their use of the network of enterprises. Within the chapter, Audrey Fairgrieve, Beth Curtis, Dr Gary Husband, Elizabeth Draper, Heather Booth-Martin, Jason Boucher, Kerry E Heathcote, and Toby Doncaster share their insights.

REFERENCES

Gruber, H. E., and Wallace, D. B. (1999) 'The case study method and evolving systems approach for understanding unique creative people at work' in Sternberg, R. J. (ed.) *Handbook of creativity*. New York: Cambridge University Press, pp. 93–115.

Wallace, D. B., and Gruber, H. E. (1989) *Creative people at work: Twelve cognitive case studies*. New York: Oxford University Press.

CHAPTER ONE

Multifaceted identities

VIGNETTE: HATS

People say teachers wear many hats. I remember the first time I came across this concept during my teacher training. Sometimes I think it might be easier to literally have a different hat for each role I embody. At least then I might know who I am or who I am expected to be, and when. The only problem is, I'm an artist some of the time and I'm not sure I could pull off a beret.

Cairns, A. (2024) Accidental. Unpublished vignette.

INTRODUCTION

This chapter introduces the concept of multifaceted identities and what this term means for vocational and technical FE teachers and trainers in the UK. This chapter begins by explaining the term before drawing on the work of educationalist Sarah Steadman (2023) to situate it within an educational context. This chapter also draws on four key areas outlining multifaceted identities, widely and more specifically concerning FE teachers and trainers: (1) the idea that teachers and trainers are assemblages of many identities, (2) identity flux, (3) communities of practice (CoP), and (4) professional locations.

This chapter predominately draws on the work of researchers writing on the topic of teachers and trainers and multifaceted identities. Reference is made to the works of Barkhuizen (2016) whose research reflects on language teacher identity; Kong (2018) whose research is focused on the identities of bilingual teachers of English; Rutstein-Riley et al. (2019) write on identity and lifelong learning in Higher Education; Schutz et al. (2020) who write on teacher identity development; Bucura (2022) who is concerned about music teacher identity; and Menter (2023) who writes on teacher educator identity.

> **TRY THIS! MINDFUL JOURNALING**
>
> Set aside a few minutes to write down your thoughts on your professional identity and reflective practice. Consider which aspects of your professional identity you find most challenging to navigate in your teaching or training role, and how reflection helps you better understand and embrace your multifaceted professional identity.

PART 1: MULTIFACETED IDENTITIES

Within this book, multifaceted identities are understood in terms of professional identity. They are a complex mix of diverse enterprises that come together to build a sense of self. Each of us is made up of numerous enterprises that change over time; however, multifaceted identities must not be confused with intersectionality. The intersections of our identities encompass social categories including ethnicity, social class, and gender that overlap and are often discussed in terms of discrimination and/or disadvantage. With multifaceted identities, rather than a singular professional identity tied to one profession or enterprise, we are defined by several identities that interact. These multiple professions come together to build our overall sense of self.

In *Identity: Keywords in Teacher Education* (2023) Sarah Steadman outlines that we all have multiple interconnected identities, each informed by our histories, culture, and location. To have a multifaceted identity is to hold more than one identity at a time, distinct also from dual identities (see Section 2), those with multiple identities have three or more identities that they resonate with. Many of us will have multiple identities at any one time, but outwardly we might choose one dominant way to identify; this is often due to the concept of multifaceted identities presenting as a complex one and the notion that identifying as more than one profession is difficult to do unambiguously (Menter, 2023). To overcome this, psychologist Dan McAdams (2012) suggests that we often choose to identify in one way to simplify what is otherwise a quite complex conundrum. This is true for vocational and technical FE teachers and trainers, who might present a unified professional identity outwardly but who are contending with integrating other (sub)identities internally (Schutz et al., 2020).

Sub-identities might include other roles within FE such as leadership or mentoring roles, and/or quality roles. For example, when stopped in a shop by an old acquaintance, how much easier is it to answer the question, 'what is it that you do?' with, 'I'm a teacher,' rather than, in my case, the more accurate 'I'm an artist-teacher-researcher.' McAdams (2012) makes the point that in the modern world we inhabit we are expected to be and act in a multitude of ways, and as vocational or technical FE teachers or trainers, we live this experience. We are the embodiment of a collection of roles, rather than one whole (Bucura, 2022). As FE teachers and trainers, we might be expected to be vocational or technical experts as well as seasoned pedagogues.

Vocational and technical FE teachers and trainers are a prime example of professionals that it can be reasonably expected to have a multifaceted identity. As we travel through our professional lives, we acquire knowledge, skills, and experience from different enterprise: from our days as vocational or technical students, as artists/hairdressers/mechanics/chefs, as student-teacher, and as FE teachers and trainers. Storm and Martin (2022) describe this as teachers and trainers becoming assemblages of all their previous and current experiences, an assemblage or *agencement* is a concept originally presented in the work of Gilles Deleuze and Félix Guattari, defined as "a collection of things which have been gathered together or assembled" (1980), often displayed in rhizomes. Rhizomatic mapping is a powerful tool that can be used for navigating the complexities of professional identity as well as knowledge and social relations. FE teacher and trainer assemblages can be visualised in rhizomatic maps, showing how identity is made up of numerous different sub-identities. In this act, we could also consider how our professional identities might be broken down further and consider, for example, how as an FE teacher or trainer you may also have responsibility related to being an expert in wider curricular demands, such as meeting minimum core, employability and personal development behaviours and welfare (PDBW) demands (Cooney, 2015), and how vocational and technical roles might require you to take control of admin responsibilities. In contrast to other mapping techniques you may have engaged in, rhizomatic maps avoid the use of a centre point and discrete categories and instead have multiple entry and exit points. This way of mapping helps to remove the hierarchal nature often present in mapping activities. Due to this, the rhizomatic maps allow for connections between any two points or professional identities to be made. Rhizomes are flexible and dynamic and rhizomatic maps are no different, they can highlight new professional identities or transformation of existing ones, through the connections and interactions within the map. Rhizomatic maps are in constant flux, meaning they are ideal for exploring complex phenomena, such as professional identity.

While this book focuses on professional teacher and trainer identity, we also juggle this with personal ways of being; we might also be parents, partners, and/or caregivers (Rutstein-Riley et al., 2019). Writing two decades after McAdams (1993) it seems clear that his statement only becomes more accurate as we advance forward and are expected to be more and more things. With this realisation we should note that the interplay between identities is often dynamic and sometimes conflicted (Kong, 2018).

> ### *TRY THIS!* THE FE TEACHER OR TRAINER ASSEMBLAGE
>
> Consider yourself as an FE teacher or trainer assemblage and engage in Deleuze and Guattari's concept of rhizomatic mapping (1980). Write each of your identities down and link them with lines. In presenting your identity in this way, it allows you to view your multiple identities without hierarchy and with fluidity. In mapping your professional identities visually, you will be able to acknowledge connections and intersections between them. You may be able to take notes of how your different professional identities intertwine and influence each other and look at my teacher assemblage as a rhizomatic map below to see how my multiple professional identities interact with each other (Figure 1.1)
>
>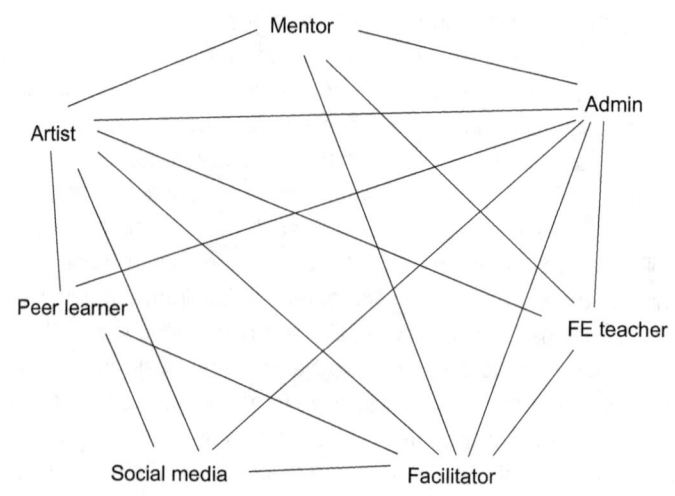
>
> **FIGURE 1.1** My FE teacher assemblage as a rhizomatic map.

PART 2: IDENTITY FLUX

Our multifaceted identities are not rigid (Mentor, 2023), are instead in constant flux (Adams, 2007), and are susceptible to change over time (Kong, 2018).

Therefore, it is unlikely that the professions and/or enterprises that you hold today are the same as the ones you held ten years ago or as the ones you will hold ten years from now. It is worth noting that you might experience identity flux far more regular than every decade and could be a regular as changing daily, particularly if you find yourself working in different professional locations regularly (Cairns, 2023). Additionally, as you develop your professional identities, over time you will start to change your idea of yourself (Fejes and Köpsén, 2014). These changes can be linked to changing personal beliefs and value systems, and external changes to your vocational or technical FE teaching or training landscapes (Steadman, 2023).

McAdams (1993) outlines that identities are unlikely to ever be fully achieved and that our professional identity is likely to continue to change throughout our adult lives, as we continue to encounter new experiences, such as taking on a new role (Menter, 2023). For FE teachers and trainers, there might be very clear new experiences and/or moments of change in professional identity, such as enrolling in or completing an initial teacher training course (Menter, 2023) or starting your first position in FE. Education is transformative (Mezirow, 1990; Illeris, 2014), and transformative education can take place in any context where the learning changes elements of your identity and sense of self (Illeris, 2014), contexts can include but are not limited to formal education as well as CPD and professional learning activities. Identity is likely to shift between contexts, as depending on the one you find yourself situated in, there may be a need for you to embody more of one part of your multifaceted than another (Steadman, 2023). In shifting professional identity to respond to context, vocational and technical FE teachers and trainers move from one professional identity to another or somewhere in between (Fejes and Köpsén, 2014).

As well as context, you might also find that your professional identity is shaped by those around you, as identity is often socially constructed (McAdams, 1993; Barkhuizen, 2016). Specifically, teacher and trainer identity has been shown to be socially situated, with situated relationships between yourself and other persons influencing the dynamic nature of your professional identity (Steadman, 2023). Vocational and technical FE teacher and trainer identity is constantly in flux due to the changing nature of education and relationships between learner and teacher, teacher and learner, and teacher to their vocation (Thornton, 2011). This might mean that you identify more strongly with your vocation when with other vocationalists and more like an FE teacher or trainer when with other FE teachers or trainers. Adams (2007) suggests that this is due to the social world you find yourself in contributing to how you identify, with the fluid, dynamic nature of multifaceted identities allows for this (Barkhuizen, 2016).

> ### TRY THIS! FEELING LIKE AN FE TEACHER OR TRAINER
>
> Pinpoint the moment you felt like an FE teacher or trainer by answering the questions provided below. It might be useful to consider the construction of your FE teacher identity. This activity will be particularly beneficial for those who are pre-service educators as you can reflect on this in real-time and notice moments of change (Bucura, 2022).

- **Background Questions:**
    - Can you recall a specific instance or event where you felt like you were truly teaching or training in an FE setting?
    - What were the circumstances surrounding that moment?
    - How did you feel during that moment?
    - What were you doing at that time that made you feel like an FE teacher or trainer?
- **Contextual Questions:**
    - Can you describe the environment or setting where this moment occurred?
    - Were there any learners or groups of learners involved?
    - What subject or topic were you teaching at that time?
- **Professional Development Questions:**
    - Did this moment align with any specific teaching or training strategies or methodologies you had learned or practised?
    - How did this moment contribute to your growth as an FE teacher or trainer?
    - Did you receive any feedback or recognition for your teaching or training during this moment?
- **Impact Questions:**
    - How did this moment impact your learners?
    - Did it lead to any changes in your teaching or training approach or philosophy?
    - Did it influence your career trajectory or aspirations as an FE teacher or trainer?
- **Personal Reflection Questions:**
    - How did this moment align with your personal values or beliefs about teaching or training?
    - Did it reinforce your passion for teaching or training in the FE sector?
    - How has this moment shaped your identity as an FE teacher or trainer?
- **Future Implications Questions:**
    - How do you think this moment will influence your future teaching or training practices?

- Are there any lessons or insights from this moment that you plan to carry forward in your FE teaching or training career?
- How do you envision your role as an FE teacher or trainer evolving based on this experience?

PART 3: COMMUNITIES OF PRACTICE

Leaving and entering CoP can also be transformative (Lave and Wenger, 1991). CoPs bring together groups of people who share a concern or a passion for the same area of interest. They are held together by three pillars: domain, community, and practice; the domain refers to what the CoP encompasses and helps to build a shared understanding; community focuses on how the CoP operates, how relationships are managed, and how growth is approached; and practice refers to the knowledge and skills of the CoP and how these are effectively communicated to members.

You might find that moving from your vocational or technical CoP to an FE CoP contributes to feeling unsettled in your identity, this is because you are experiencing a demanding transformation (Wenger, 2000). In this transition you are developing a pedagogised identity, where previously you held a vocationalist or technical one (Shreeve, 2009; Page, 2012). We might experience this early in our careers when still training to become teachers or trainers, or we might experience it sometime later. For vocational and technical teachers and trainers, we may transform our vocational or technical identity into a multifaceted professional identity by linking our new teacher or trainer identity to a familiar one (Mezirow, 1991). Depending on where you are in your FE career you may have found or you may go on to find that the transformation from vocationalist or technicalist to teacher or trainer happens relatively quickly, this is due to teacher training courses often being relatively short and more intensive than other courses you may have studied in relation to your vocational or technical area (Adams, 2007).

It should be noted that the transformative nature of education does not stop at moving from a vocational or technical identity to a teacher or trainer identity. We may also experience a shift between student-teacher identity and teacher identity post-initial teacher training (Schutz et al., 2020). Additionally, those of us who move into the role of teacher-educator are likely to experience an identity shift from teacher to teacher-educator. These three shifts are examples of boundary crossing (Wenger, 2000). Boundary crossing occurs when an individual is a member of several CoPs and stays on the edges of each, such as a vocational or technical CoP and FE teacher or trainer CoP (Wenger, 2000). Remaining on the periphery of many CoPs allows you multi-membership and an ability to build and sustain connections between them (Fejes and Köpsén). Additionally, this allows you to take knowledge from one CoP and apply it to another in an act of brokering (Wenger, 2000). Brokering allows us to engage with members of vocational or technical CoP and FE teacher or trainer CoP seamlessly and becomes important if you wish to keep a connection to your vocational or technical area and its community, once you acquire your teacher or trainer identity (Wenger, 2000).

Due to the identity flux we experience our professional lives can be full of change. However, it is likely that you will also experience periods of relative stability in your professional identity (McAdams, 1993). These times of stability may last months, years, or longer and will allow you time and space to enjoy your renewed sense of self (Erikson, 1994). However, in terms of identity awareness, you are likely to be most aware of the identity, or identities, you hold during the moments of transition (1994). It should be noted that major life events, including marriage or divorce, having a child, moving house/location, death, menopause, and retirement, can also impact identity more widely (McAdams, 1993). While these events are not directly related to your professional life, they may result in reflection or change in life direction that you take. You may find that the most powerful tool for transforming identity comes from within, with hooks (1994) suggesting that we can change, or transform, our identities by changing how we think about ourselves, the activities in this book are intended to give you space to reflect and consider how you think about yourself and to empower you to make any changes you see fit.

> ### *TRY THIS!* YOUR MEMBERSHIP IN COP
>
> Explore your multi-membership in CoP using a reproduction of Wenger et al. (2002) degrees of community participant figure. There are three types of membership you can hold within any CoP: core, active, and peripheral. Your engagement in the community becomes progressively looser as you move from core engagement to peripheral (Wenger, 2000). If you hold core membership in a community, you are likely to be highly engaged in it and have extensive knowledge and experience related to the domain. If you hold active membership, your knowledge and experience might vary in level; however, you are likely to still be engaged in the community and with other members of the community. If you hold peripheral membership, you are likely to contribute less to the community. You may be a peripheral member as you are new to the community, in which instance your membership may grow as your knowledge and expertise develops.

However, you may have peripheral membership for other reasons, such as being engaged in multiple communities. With multi-membership your engagement is likely to be sporadic or limited to observing the activities of the group due to the logistics of holding multiple memberships.

Consider the CoP that you have engagement with and decide which type of membership you hold in each. I have provided my own degrees of community participation (Figure 1.2) to help guide you in this activity. As membership to CoP can impact identity, this activity will be useful when assessing how significant each professional identity is to you and your overarching professional identity. Be aware that membership is not static, and your answers today may differ next week, next month, or next year.

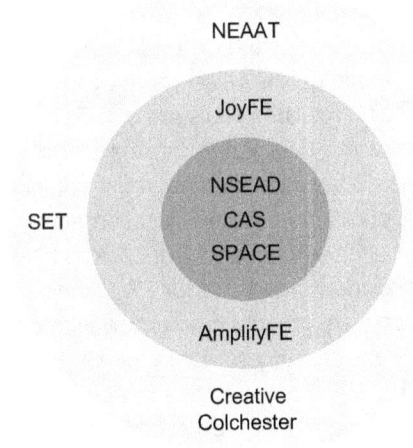

FIGURE 1.2 My degrees of community participation (Wenger et al., 2002).

PART 4: PROFESSIONAL LOCATION

As an FE teacher or trainer, with a multifaceted identity, and membership in multiple CoP, you may have experienced feeling pulled in different directions by the different professional identities that you hold or of feeling confused by which professional identity to prioritise (Cribb et al., 2009). Context is one of the factors that influences how we identify, and there are two ways to consider context in relation to professional location: the first aligns with Briggs (2007) and his notion that professional location as not a physical location, but the profession that you belong to. However, for others, professional location does refer to physical settings related to each profession (Page, 2012). In either instance, professional locations come with their own values, attitudes, and norms (Gilmore and Hatcher, 2023), and you may find that these differ between each professional location. Understanding this might help remedy feelings of identity confusion or conflict (Brooks, 2016; Kong, 2018).

FE is vast and across a career in the sector you may find yourself working for different providers. While changing professional location might be subtle, such as moving from one FE provider to another, changing jobs can have a significant impact on your professional identity, as your context and community change. Identity shifts happen in moments of transition, career progression (Vella, 2016), and moving to a new role – even if it is the same as your previous role – is still a moment of change (Gilmore and Hatcher, 2023). Additionally, changes within your current workplace can impact your professional identity, positively or negatively (Brooks, 2016), including, for example, changes at different management levels within your educational institutions (Brooks, 2016). These changes might come about due to larger changes, such as changes to government, which is likely to result in new educational policy (Winch, 2017) as well as redirecting of public funding, either away from or towards FE (Groves, 2015). Changes to professional standards in FE may also impact your professional teacher or trainer identity. Depending on when you started in FE you may have experienced this once, or more, with FE experiencing the introduction of three sets of standards to which the FE teacher or trainer must conform to since the early 2000s, with the latest published by the Education and Training Foundation (ETF) in 2022. These began with the now-debunked Lifelong Learning UK (LLUK) in 2007, which provided standards for FE teachers and trainers (Plowright and Barr, 2012), which were brought in to improve the quality of teaching and learning within the FE and training sector in the UK (Department for Education and Skills, 2006). The ETF continued this work when LLUK disbanded and in 2014 backed by the government they published their Professional Standards for Teachers and Trainers (ETF, 2014). These standards were then updated in June 2022. The ETFs professional standards set out the roles and responsibilities of teachers and trainers in the FE sector, under three domains: *professional skills*, *professional values and attributes, and professional knowledge and understanding* (ETF, 2022). Described by the ETF as fundamental to teachers and trainers, it is likely that adherence to these standards, and changes and updates to them, will impact your professional identity.

Additionally, the professional standards may impact your professional identity as standard eight promotes continued engagement in your subject specialism (2022), supporting the idea of holding a multifaceted professional identity. The impact of this on you is the expectation that you will continue to engage in your vocational or technical identity once you teach or train in FE. The ETF outlines that this engagement is an expectation, not a 'nice to have' (2022). Professional standard twenty is also pertinent to what we are discussing within this book, with continued engagement in several CoPs encouraged, including those related to your vocation, to allow you to facilitate enrichment and developmental opportunities for learners within these communities (2022).

As we experience changes in our working environments, due to changing jobs or outside factors such as educational reforms (Briggs, 2007; Taubman, 2015), we must react by reshaping our professional identities (Rutstein-Riley et al., 2019). Reshaping our professional identity will allow us to continue developing our roles in line with any new or changing expectations in values and standards. We must try to adapt our multifaceted professional identity to meet new benchmarks or face no longer fitting into the community associated with it (Wenger, 2000). We might also notice that our identity transitions as our careers change over a lifetime (Bucura, 2022); this is because teacher and training identity is never complete and is fluid enough to change across time as well as context (Kong, 2018). At any one time you will be negotiating your multiple identities and sub-identities, including your vocational or technical identity (Menter, 2023), membership to CoPs and their relationships to each other (Barkhuizen, 2016). While identity is often constructed socially, there may be times when you find your existence as an FE teacher or training contests what others believe being an FE teacher or trainer to be, as most people you encounter will have their own understanding of the identity (Menter, 2023). This might be problematic if their understanding comes from the idea of a compulsory educator. Contradictions may also come from existing multiple professional locations (Barkhuizen, 2016; Kong, 2018; Schutz et al., 2020). Additionally, vocational, technical, and other sub-identities might easily contest your teacher identity as what it means to be a teacher is tightly bound to context (Thornton, 2011).

TRY THIS! MOMENTS OF ADJUSTMENT

Reflect on any time(s) you have had to adjust your professional identity to fit into changing expectations, in your vocation or technical area, teaching or training, or both. Use the questions below to guide your thinking.

- **Background Questions:**
    - What were the circumstances surrounding that particular moment?
    - How did you emotionally respond during that instance of professional identity adjustment?
    - What actions were you taking at that time that required you to adapt your professional identity, either as a vocationalist or technicalist or as a teacher or trainer?

- **Contextual Questions:**
  - Could you paint a picture of the environment or setting where this moment of identity adjustment took place?
  - Were there specific people involved in this scenario?
- **Professional Development Questions:**
  - In what ways did this experience contribute to your growth and development as a teacher or trainer within the FE sector?
  - Were there any feedback or recognition you received regarding your handling of this situation?
- **Impact Questions:**
  - How did this moment of professional identity adjustment impact you, if at all?
  - Did it prompt any changes in your teaching or training methods or philosophical approach?
  - Has this experience influenced your career trajectory or aspirations within the FE domain?
- **Personal Reflection Questions:**
  - How did this instance of adjusting your professional identity resonate with your personal values or beliefs about teaching or training?
  - In what ways has this event shaped your sense of identity as an FE teacher or trainer?
- **Future Implications Questions:**
  - Are there particular lessons or insights from this instance that you intend to carry forward in your teaching or training career?
  - How do you foresee your role as an FE teacher or trainer evolving based on the lessons learned from this experience?

CONCLUSION

To conclude multifaceted identities can be understood as a complex mix of diverse enterprises that come together to build a sense of self. We have seen how having a multifaceted identity may be a complicated place to find yourself. Reflective practice is highly encouraged throughout your career to help you continue to transform your professional identities and to navigate the identity flux you might experience, take this as a sign to remain engaged in regular reflection. This chapter has shown that you may find within your teacher or trainer professional identity, you hold multiple sub-identities, including those of vocational or technical area and pedagogical expert (Barkhuizen, 2016), and that you are expected to be committed to maintaining and developing expertise in each, with multi-membership to CoPs (Turner, McKenzie, Stone, 2009). Juggling these sub-identities and the responsibilities that come with them can be difficult but negotiating time spent in each professional location can help. In the next chapter, we explore what the network of enterprises is and why it is important in relation to vocational and technical FE teacher and trainer multifaceted professional identities.

REFERENCES

Adams, J. (2007) 'Artists becoming teachers: Expressions of identity transformation in a virtual forum', *International Journal of Art & Design Education*, 26(3), pp. 264–273. doi: 10.1111/j.1476-8070.2007.00537.x.

Barkhuizen, G. (2016) *Reflections on language teacher identity research*. Abingdon: Taylor & Francis.

Briggs, A. R. J. (2007) 'Exploring professional identities: Middle leadership in further education colleges', *School Leadership and Management*, 27(5), pp. 471–485. doi: 10.1080/13632430701606152.

Brooks, C. (2016) *Teacher subject identity in professional practice: Teaching with a professional compass*. New York: Routledge.

Bucura, E. (2022) *Music teacher identities: Places, people, and practices of the professional self*. Münster: Waxmann Verlag GmbH.

Cairns, A. (2023) *Interrogating artist-teacher identity transformation in adult community learning*. Doctoral thesis, Norwich University of the Arts.

Cooney, R. (2015) *What does FE professionalism look like? How should it be achieved? And how should FE professionals make their voices heard?* Available at: https://feweek.co.uk/2015/07/13/professional-questions-on-fe-teaching-amid-coasting-colleges-warning-at-atl-vocational-conference/ (Accessed 29 March 2023).

Cribb, A., Hextall, I., Mahony, P., and Gewirtz, S. (2009) *Changing teacher professionalism: International trends, challenges and ways forward*. London: Routledge.

Deleuze, G., and Guattari, F. (1987) *A thousand plateaus*. Trans. Brian Massumi. Minneapolis, MN: University of Minnesota Press.

Department for Education and Skills (2006) *Further education: Raising skills, improving life chances*. London: The Stationery Office.

Education and Training Foundation (ETF) https://www.et-foundation.co.uk/professional-standards/teachers/ https://www.et-foundation.co.uk/supporting/support-practitioners/professional-standards/ (Accessed 28 March 2023).

Education and Training Foundation (ETF) (2022) *Professional standards for teachers and trainers in the further education and training Sector*. Available at: https://set.et-foundation.co.uk/your-career/the-professional-standards/the-20-professional-standards-to-enhance-your-practice. (Accessed 8 July 2022).

Erikson, E. (1994) *Identity and the life cycle*. New York: W. W. Norton & Company.

Fejes, A., and Köpsén, S. (2014) 'Vocational teachers' identity formation through boundary crossing', *Journal of Education and Work*, 27(3), pp. 265–283. dio: 10.1080/13639080.2012.742181.

Gilmore, J., and Hatcher, M. (2023) *Preparing for college and university teaching: Competencies for graduate and professional students*. New York: Routledge.

Groves, B. E. (2015) 'Teaching and ideology, Or why aren't we all dancing? A personal view' in Daley, M., Orr, K., and Petrie, J. (eds) *Further education and the twelve dancing princesses*. London: UCL IOE Press, p. 25.

hooks, b. (1994) *Teaching to transgress: Education as the practice of freedom*. New York: Routledge.

Illeris, K. (2014) *Transformative learning and identity*. London: Routledge.

Kong, M. (2018) *The hopes and experiences of bilingual teachers of English: Investments, expectations and identity*. Abingdon: Taylor & Francis.

Lave, J., and Wenger, E. (1991) *Situated learning: Legitimate peripheral participation*. Cambridge: Cambridge University Press.

McAdams, D. P. (2012). Exploring psychological themes through life narrative accounts. In J. A. Holstein, and J. F. Gubrium (eds.), *Varieties of narrative analysis*. Thousand Oaks, California: Sage, pp. 15–32.

Menter, I. (2023) *The Palgrave handbook of teacher education research*. Cham: Springer International Publishing.

Mezirow, J. (1990) *Fostering critical reflection in adulthood*. Jossey-Bass: San Francisco.

Mezirow, J. (1991) *Transformative dimensions of adult learning*. San Francisco: Jossey-Bass.

Page, T. (2012) 'A shared place of discovery and creativity: Practices of contemporary art and design pedagogy', *International Journal for Art and Design Education*, 31(1), pp. 67–77. doi: 10.1111/j.1476-8070.2012.01732.x.

Plowright, D., and Barr, G. (2012) 'An integrated professionalism in further education: A time for phronesis?', *Journal of Further and Higher Education,* 36(1), pp. 1–16. doi: 10.1080/0309877X.2011.590584.

Rutstein-Riley, A., Gammel, J. A., and Motulsky, S. (2019) *Identity and lifelong learning in higher education*. Charlotte, NC: Information Age Publishing, Incorporated.

Schutz, P. A., Hong, J., and Francis, D. C. (2020) *Teachers' goals, beliefs, emotions, and identity development: Investigating complexities in the profession*. New York: Routledge.

Shreeve, A. (2009) '"I'd rather be seen as a practitioner, come in to teach my subject": Identity work in part-time art and design tutors', *International Journal of Art & Design Education*, 28(2), pp. 151–159. doi: 10.1111/j.1476-8070.2009.01602.x.

Steadman, S. (2023) *Identity: Keywords in teacher education*. London: Bloomsbury Academic.

Storm, J. K., and Martin, D. A. (2022) 'Towards a critical posthuman understanding of teacher development and practice: A multi-case study of beginning teachers', *Teaching and Teacher Education,* p. 114. doi: 10.1016/j.tate.2022.103688

Taubman, D. (2015) 'Reframing professionalism and reclaiming the dance' in Daley, M., Orr, K., and Petrie, J. (eds) *Further education and the twelve dancing princesses*. London, pp. 107–119.

Thornton, A. (2011) 'Being an artist teacher: A liberating identity?', *International Journal of Art & Design Education*, 30(1), pp. 31–36. doi: 10.1111/j.1476-8070.2011.01684.x.

Turner, R., McKenzie, L. and Stone, M. (2009) Square peg – round hole: The emerging professional identities of HE in FE lecturers working in a partner college network in south-west England. *Research in Post-Compulsory Education*, 14.

Vella, R. (2016) *Artist-teachers in context: International dialogues.* Rotterdam, The Netherlands: Brill | Sense (Doing Arts Thinking: Arts Practice, Research and Education).

Wenger, E. (2000) *Communities of practice: Learning meaning and identity.* Cambridge: University of Cambridge Press.

Wenger, E., McDermott, R. A., and Snyder, W. (2002) *Cultivating communities of practice: A guide to managing mnowledge.* Boston: Harvard Business School Press.

Winch, E. (2017) *What impact with the snap general election have on educational reforms.* Available at https://forms.ncfe.org.uk/blog/2017/4/20/what-impact-will-snap-general-election-have-on-education-reforms/ (Accessed 11 March 2024).

CHAPTER TWO

What is a network of enterprises and why is it important?

> **VIGNETTE: NAMING ENTERPRISES**
>
> I name my enterprises and am surprised by how many different things I am. I muse, 'no wonder I'm tired, no wonder there is no time.' The answer is right in front of me, displayed in a series of ebbs and flows. Thick black blocks not to be mistaken. I've taken too much on and now I must decide; Who am I? What is significant? And what can be left behind?
>
> Cairns, A. (2024) Naming enterprises. Unpublished vignette.

INTRODUCTION

In this chapter, the network of enterprises will be introduced and its importance to vocational and technical FE teachers and trainers will be explored. By the end of this chapter, you will be thoroughly informed about the tool and be in a better position to engage in its use. The tool will be outlined, and its early use and history drawing on the work of American psychologists Doris Wallace and Howard Gruber (1989) shared. This chapter also provides a case study of the use of the network of enterprises from the published literature, which explores James Daichendt's (2011) use of the tool with artist-teacher George Wallis. This chapter ends by outlining the limitations of the tool before suggesting how an updated version of the network of enterprises goes some way to overcome them.

PART 1: NETWORK OF ENTERPRISES

Part 1 explores the main themes of networks of enterprises, drawing on the work of Wallace and Gruber (1989). This includes the original use of and purpose of the network of enterprises, the importance of goals to the tool, how the significance of involvement in each enterprise works, and the role community plays, with reference to Wenger (2000).

The main purpose of the network of enterprises is to provide a simplified overview of an individual's engagement in different enterprises, to highlight the patterns of continuity and the relationships between enterprises (Gruber and Wallace, 1999). The network of enterprises comes with the assumption that you will be engaged in some way with the community connected to each of your enterprises (Wallace and Gruber, 1989) and that you will have access to the network and cultural resources of these communities (Gruber, 1981). This notion draws on the work of Lave and Wenger's community of practice (CoP) (1991) and engagement in the domain, community, and practice of the community.

Use and purpose

Networks of enterprises are a tool first used by American psychologists Doris Wallace and Howard Gruber (1989) with creative people at work. I note here that while Wallace and Gruber's work was aimed towards creative people, it is clear the reach of this tool goes far beyond a traditional understanding of the term *creative people*, as this book shows, with Gruber (1981) using the network of enterprises to explore the creative work of Charles Darwin, a figure better known for his work on the theory of evolution, rather than his creativity. The network of enterprises is not only suitable for artists or musicians but for any professional who engages in multiple enterprises and acts creatively in their work, such as vocational and technical FE teachers and trainers. Wallace and Gruber (1989) outline creative people as those who engage in work that is purposeful and social in nature. FE teaching and training is both purposeful and social (Steadman, 2023), making FE teachers and trainers creative people.

As a tool, the network of enterprise can help us to define our professional selves (Wallace and Gruber, 1989), by tracking and charting our enterprise over time (Gruber and Wallace, 1999). The tool has an emphasis on documenting prolonged periods, with the belief that the work creative people do takes time to achieve (1989). Wallace and Gruber (1989) outlined enterprises as any activities that required your attention and involvement, and this can include your career(s) (vocational, technical, and/or pedagogical), hobbies, or even being engaged as a student. The enterprises that creative people choose to engage in give their life purpose (McAdams, 1993).

The design of the network of enterprises enables us to document the ebbs and flows of our enterprises over time (Steadman, 2023), allowing us to build a picture of our unique professional identities and life stories (McAdams, 1993). As our involvement in enterprises changes over time, our professional identities also change in corresponding ways. Networks of enterprises also show our commitment to our creative work. Wallace and Gruber (1989) suggest that creative work is not easy, and thus not undertaken by everyone, and this is true for the work of vocational and technical FE teachers and trainers, with recruitment and retention being an ongoing issue in the FE sector (DfE, 2018).

Networks of enterprises help to document how our professional lives diverge as our careers expand and time passes, as life goes on you may find that you acquire more enterprises (Wallace and Gruber, 1989). This is particularly pertinent for vocational and technical FE teachers and trainers, who experience this divergence when entering FE. I believe that networks of enterprises are an ideal tool for FE teachers and trainers, as it captures the pluralistic nature of the multifaceted professional role seamlessly. Wallace and Gruber (1989) outline that we can take knowledge from one enterprise and apply it to another, that insight in one area may reawaken another enterprise we are currently less significantly involved in, and that skills may be transferable across boundaries (Wenger, 2000). This is often seen with vocational and technical FE teachers and trainers, who are expected to bring their subject knowledge and experiences into the classroom (ETF, 2022).

Goal achievement

Networks of enterprises have a focus on goal achievement, and Wallace and Gruber (1989) believed that by documenting your enterprises on the tool you can better see how involvement in enterprises helps individuals to works towards goals in different areas. For vocational and technical FE teachers and trainers this might mean the ability to continue working towards professional goals related to their vocational or technical career as well as their FE teaching or training career and other possible enterprises such as continued study. A focus on goal achievement in different areas allows you to keep engaged, helping you to embrace your multifaceted professional identity. The enterprises documented on your network of enterprises are your main lines of activity; however, you might have other activities that you do not include that fall outside of this. It should be noted that an enterprise might not start as a main line but may become one as its importance in your professional identity grows. However, your chosen main-line enterprises are usually relatively permanent features in your professional life (Wallace and Gruber, 1989). This is in line with the idea that we tend to have and experience relatively stable senses of identity (McAdams,

1993), and completed networks of enterprises makes this continuity clear (Gruber and Wallace, 1999).

The main advantage of having several main lines is that if you find yourself stuck or not progressing in one, you may be able to move forward in another, ensuring that your productivity does not come to a complete stop and allowing goal achievement in different areas to continue (Wallace and Gruber, 1989). Additionally, it means that when you re-engage in an enterprise after a break, you resume the activity without having to start from the beginning (Gruber and Wallace, 1999). As you engage with the tool, your network of enterprises becomes a personalised, individualised picture, which can tell the story of your professional life (McAdams, 1993). The tool shows you as a complex, unique, organised system of enterprises (Wallace and Gruber, 1989) and helps us to see how our multiple enterprises create a sense of a unified professional identity that integrates our sub-identities (Schutz et al., 2020). Gruber (1981) states that in this process we are each seen as a unique host of a network of enterprises.

Significance of involvement

Within a network of enterprises, your enterprises are organised in columns and the width of these communicates your level of involvement in each, from no involvement to significant involvement. This tool is well placed to document how you organise your time and resources, with the process of charting allowing you to make visual the trade-off between your enterprises (Wallace and Gruber, 1989). The trade-off refers to how involvement in one enterprise impacts your involvement in another, for a vocational or technical FE teacher or trainer, it might be that your involvement in teaching or training becomes so significant and that there is little room left for your vocational or technical activity. Wallace and Gruber (1989) show this kind of experience to be expected and suggest that we still maintain a low level of participation in enterprises that are currently not of significant interest to us, by monitoring the activities of the attached community, while not actively engaging in them. This relates to Wenger et al's (2002) work on degrees of community participation and would place you as having a peripheral membership to the community attached to the enterprise you currently have no to little involvement with. Membership can change as significance of involvement increases, allowing you to make a more substantial contribution to the community (Wallace and Gruber, 1989), and this would see you move towards being an active or core member of the community you were previously monitoring (Wenger et al., 2002).

Reviewing your involvement in each enterprise allows you to consider your professional development and career as one whole story and adjust the trade-off between enterprises as you feel appropriate (Wallace and Gruber, 1989). Related to this, it should be noted that the network of enterprises highlights the legitimacy of having multiple enterprises, allowing for the level of involvement of each enterprise to be stated in each period. Wallace and Gruber (1989) suggest a particular benefit of multiple enterprises is the ability to move between them and act according to your changing moods and interests, with different enterprises requiring different things from you at different times. This allows you to choose and shape your own professional identity and your direction of travel in the future (Wallace and Gruber, 1989).

PART 2: EARLY USE AND A CASE STUDY FROM THE PUBLISHED LITERATURE

Wallace and Gruber (1999) provide several case studies of networks of enterprises including of naturalist, geologist, and biologist Charles Darwin (Gruber, 1981), psychologist Jean Piaget, and theoretical physicist Albert Einstein (Gruber and Wallace, 1999). Each of these outlines the creative persons' work posthumously, from the researchers' perspective (Gruber and Wallace, 1999). Others have used the network of enterprises in the same way, including art critic and historian James Daichendt (2011) who used the tool with prominent artist, curator, and educator George Wallis. I have chosen this case study to share, over works by Wallace and Gruber, due to its relevance to vocational and technical FE teachers and trainers, with Wallis credited for his coining, and early use of the term 'artist-educator.' This term situates Wallis as a vocational teacher, albeit not one within an FE context.

Background

Gruber and Wallace (1999) and Daichendt (2011) all hold a great depth of narrative insight into the subjects of their networks of enterprises. This careful study of the individuals allows them as researchers to engage in the use of the network of enterprises; Daichendt (2011) uses a network of enterprises to draw on this knowledge and chart the life of George Wallis in his work *The Nineteenth-Century Artist-Teacher: A Case Study of George Wallis and the Creation of a New Identity.* Daichendt (2011) states that the network of enterprises is a tool that can be used to document the various facets, or enterprises, of an individual's life over time and used the tool to track Wallis' streams of thinking which resulted in his self-identification as an artist-educator. In this example, Daichendt is completing the network of enterprises on behalf of Wallis posthumously, much like Gruber's (1981) work with Charles Darwin. Daichendt (2011) uses the tool to document Wallis' entire career, highlighting his working pattern (Wallace and Gruber, 1989), I followed the same steps to complete my own network of enterprises in the style of Daichendt, pictured in Figure 2.1.

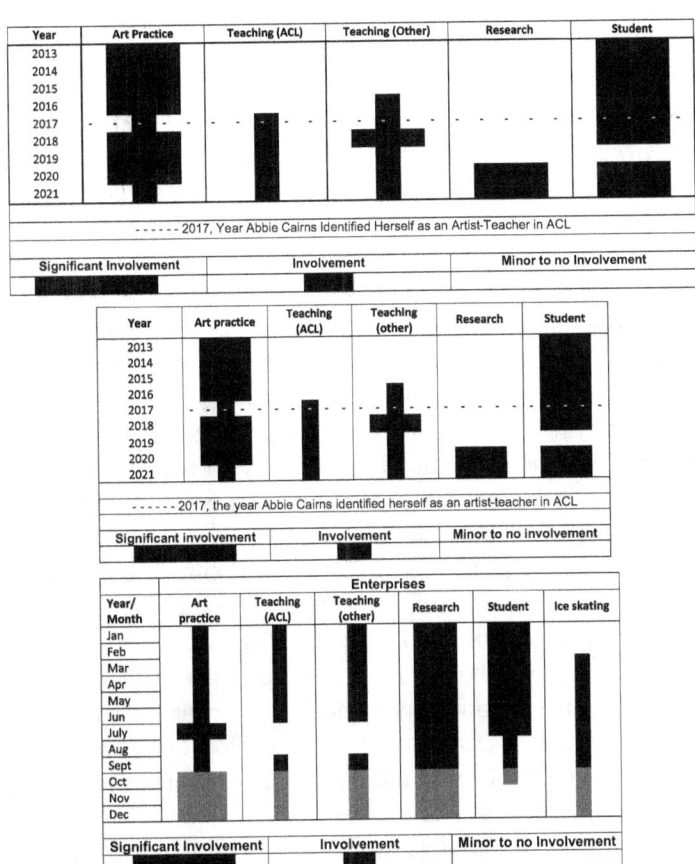

FIGURE 2.1 My network of enterprises in the style of Daichendt (Cairns, 2023).

Within his network of enterprises for Wallis, Daichendt (2011) identified five main lines; artist, teacher, philosopher, designer, and student. Access to appropriate communities related to each network is expected, no matter how limited (Gruber and Wallace, 1999). For Wallis, connections to communities varied throughout his career (Daichendt, 2009a, 2010, 2011). Wallis' engagement with the design community started at a young age, when his designer uncle adopted him after his father's death (Daichendt, 2010). While his engagement in the school community, when still a student, is said to have played a significant role in his artist-educator identity and his ideas around art and design education (Daichendt, 2009a). Wallis also engaged in communities within the British School of Design; however, his access to these communities was limited, with his ideas around teaching and curriculum rejected by colleagues, seeing him resign from the role (Daichendt, 2010). Later in his career, in 1841, Wallis joined the community associated with the Normal School, a teacher training school specifically created for the Schools of Design in England, which helped to solidify his artist-educator identity (Daichendt, 2010).

Use

Daichendt (2011) documents Wallis' enterprises in blocks of five years from 1821 to 1891. As reported earlier, creative people are often involved in several enterprises at any one time, and this was true for Wallis, with his five main lines outlined above. However, it is also documented that he spent some time as a curator and historian (Daichendt, 2011); these would have been deemed to not be main lines for Wallis from Daichendt's perspective and thus not included in the network of enterprises. It is important to note that in posthumous cases such as this, the network of enterprises can only be put together based on how the researcher(s) see the situation (Gruber and Wallace, 1999), and it might be the case that the creative person would have seen their main lines and involvement differently. From his position, Daichendt (2011) was interested in Wallis' formation of the term and concept 'artist-educator,' in 1845, seeing this naming of his identity as a creative act. The network of enterprises was intended to highlight the enterprises that led to this work over a significant period (Gruber and Wallace, 1999), and Daichendt may have found, or felt, that Wallis' involvement in curating and history did not aid this creative act. However, Daichendt (2011) did find Wallis' early experiences in his artist and designer enterprises had a deeply transformative effect on his sense of self and that engagement in these enterprises did inform his professional identity formation. Daichendt (2011) uses the tool to organise Wallis' interests throughout his life, with the network of enterprises providing a structure to map these activities visually.

Daichendt (2011) categorising Wallis' work as an artist-educator as *creative work* is important, as this feeds into the original use of the network of enterprises, with creative people at work (Wallace and Gruber, 1989). Gruber and Wallace (1999) outline that creative work must be new and add value to the related field(s). Wallis' work meets these criteria, with the adapted term 'artist-teacher' still used widely today in the field (Daichendt, 2009a, 2009b, 2010, 2011). Additionally, Wallis' work towards becoming an artist-educator was linked to his goal of improving art and design education in England (Daichendt, 2011). Wallis was committed to the educational aspects of art and design education (Daichendt, 2011), and this is thought to be a motivator for him to carry on this work over a long period (Gruber and Wallace, 1999). Further, Daichendt (2011) believes Wallis' confidence as an artist enabled him to proceed successfully as a teacher, as Wallis was able to make use of his artistic knowledge and nature to inform his teaching practice (Daichendt, 2011), in an act of boundary crossing (Wenger, 2000). At the time this was radical and saw a move away from learners copying from a master's work, towards encouraging learners to explore their individual ideas and interests (Daichendt, 2010).

Adaptations

There are differences between Gruber and Wallaces' (1999) networks of enterprises and Daichendt's (2011) use of the visual mapping tool. Daichendt (2011) made some adaptations to ensure that it was fit for his purpose. The network of enterprises used by Gruber and Wallace (1999) was designed to allow enterprises to be easily mapped onto each other and were often viewed as aerial maps (Figure 2.2). While Daichendt's network of enterprises sees a move away from aerial mapping towards a more organised table design (Figure 2.1). Due to this change, Wallis' enterprises are not mapped off each other in the same way (Daichendt, 2011). Additional notable differences include the placement of the years, from the x-axis to the y-axis, as well as the inclusion of a dotted line to highlight the year 1845, the year in which Wallis first used the term 'artist-educator' (Daichendt, 2011).

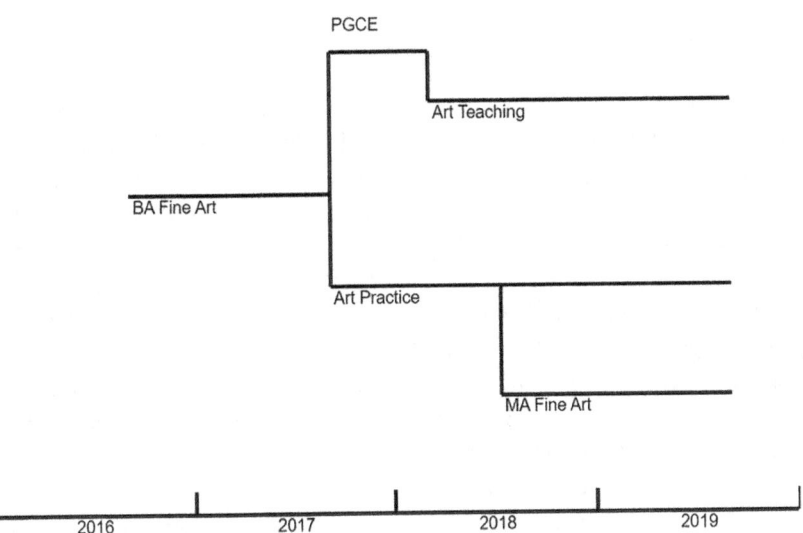

FIGURE 2.2 My Wallace and Gruber linear network of enterprise (Wallace and Gruber, 1989).

Multifaceted identity

Despite the changes, Daichendt's (2011) use of the network of enterprises still highlights Wallis' multifaceted professional identity and is used to show he was more than just an artist and an educator and he was an evolving system of enterprises (Gruber and Wallace, 1999). Daichendt's (2011) use of the tool successfully showed how Wallis' involvement in each enterprise ebbed and flowed over time (Steadman, 2023) and that the year Wallis identified himself as an artist-educator, in 1845, he was also a philosopher and designer, giving him a multifaceted identity of artist-teacher-philosopher-designer. Importantly, the completed network of enterprises shows that Wallis was never significantly involved in all his main lines at the same time; instead as significance in one area is minimised, it blooms somewhere else, with each change in involvement prompting further action, and provides the drive to keep moving forward towards goals in different areas (Gruber and Wallace, 1999). Daichendt (2011) was particularly interested in the relationship between Wallis' artist and teacher enterprises, positioning the two roles as involving an act of balance (Daichendt, 2009b), and the difficult nature of this is emphasised when Wallis gives up his full-time career as a painter to make space for the responsibilities of teaching (Daichendt, 2010). For vocational and technical FE teachers and trainers this might resonate; however, it is a clear example of when one enterprise ends, and an activity toward a goal in another area continues (Wallace and Gruber, 1989).

PART 3: LIMITATIONS AND UPDATES

The network of enterprises is not without its limitations, and Part 3 explores these along with ways to overcome them. The limitations shared draw from Wallace and Gubers' (1989) and Daichendt's (2011) use of the tool as well as my findings from my early use of the tool with artist-teachers working in adult community learning in the UK (Cairns, 2023). Part 3 covers key limitations, including the network of enterprises as a case study tool, the exclusive use of the tool with creative people, the issue of capturing flux, the legitimacy of charting historic goals, the limiting nature of naming enterprises, and the relevance of milieus. How limitations have been overcome will be covered with updates to the network of enterprises. Updates include a move to a person-centred approach, widening the use of the tool, capturing shorter periods, using the network of enterprise to plan for future involvement, empowering individuals to name their own enterprises, and the importance of accompanying narratives.

A case study tool

One of the main limitations of the network of enterprises is its exclusive use as a case study tool, to document the lives of others, often posthumously (Wallace and Gruber, 1989, Daichendt, 2011). This means the resulting networks of enterprises are always completed based on an outsider's inference, rather than lived experience (Gruber and Wallace, 1999). This places the investigator(s) or researcher(s) at the centre of the activity, rather than the individual understudy. This leaves room for subjectivity, meaning each researcher may compile a different network of enterprises for the same individual based on their preconceptions or own lived experiences. I propose that instead of use as a case study tool, the network of enterprises works best when completed by the individual understudy. With this change, the network of enterprises is completed from an insider perspective, based on the lived experience of the individual (Gruber and Wallace, 1999). This moves the network of enterprises away from a case study tool and towards that of a practical one for personal use. While this shift might appear drastic, it does not change the tool itself, with much of the network of enterprises remaining the same. The purpose of the tool does not change and remains focused on providing a simplified overview of an individual's engagement in different enterprises, the relationships between them, over time, and the importance of goal achievement (Gruber and Wallace, 1999).

Creative people

The term *creative people* might also be limiting, in terms of who the tool is available and useful to. Wallace and Grubers' (1989) understanding of a creative person might not be immediately obvious due to their understanding of the role as one that is purposeful and social. In the sense, perhaps the tool overlooks that we are or all have the capacity to be creative people and thus benefit from the tool. This widening in the audience is the second main shift that my work takes with the network of enterprises, as I open the tool up to anyone with a multifaceted identity, including vocational and technical FE teachers and trainers.

Charting flux

The charting of long periods within the network of enterprises does not adequately communicate the flux experienced by individuals (Daichendt, 2011). Despite this, the notion of prolonged periods has been seen to be central for networks of enterprises (Wallace and Gruber, 1989). This is particularly seen in Daichendt's (2011) network of enterprises for Wallis, with the five-year timeframe unable to eloquently communicate his involvement in each enterprise. Specifically, the year Wallis named himself an artist-teacher becomes overlooked and embedded with four other years that do not hold as much importance. Gruber and Wallace (1999) explore shorter periods, charting Darwin's enterprises yearly. However, it is possible to break time down into shorter durations and still do the intended job of the tool, while also capturing flux in involvement in enterprises more fully. Options include a network of enterprises that breaks down time in monthly blocks (Figure 2.3). A shorter timeframe might be easier to achieve with the move to the person-centred use of the tool, than as a case study tool. While researchers have some narrative insights into the individuals they study, this is often gleaned from diaries and published work, and this would make a month-by-month account of the individual understudy and their involvement in enterprise more difficult.

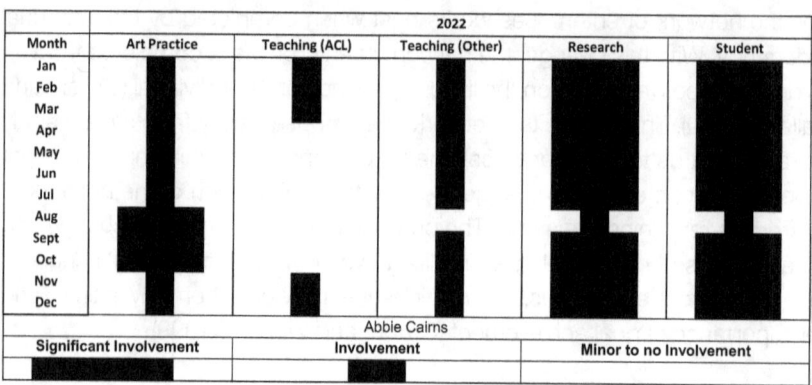

FIGURE 2.3 My monthly network of enterprises example (Cairns, 2023).

Goals

One of the main purposes of the network of enterprises is to track and chart enterprises overtime, with a focus on goal achievement (Wallace and Gruber, 1989). In the original use of the tool, goals and achievements are simply documented, often after the event, such as Wallis' goal to improve art and design education in the UK (Daichendt, 2011). Connected to this is the limitation that the researcher is working on assumptions of goals, as we cannot necessarily know what individuals' goals were, even with narrative insight (Wallace and Gruber, 1989). Goal achievement has the potential to move to being an active part of the process, undertaken by the individual understudy. With changes to the network of enterprises, it is possible to use the tool to look forward, and this allows individuals to use their network of enterprises to plan for the future by plotting how significant they want their involvement in each enterprise to be in the next one to five years. With this update to the tool, goals can be stated clearly, progress can be checked, goals can be changed, or new goals can be set once old ones are achieved. This use of the tool is in line with the idea that the network of enterprises encourages continued activity in different areas (Gruber and Wallace, 1999) and sees the network of enterprises become a tool for aspirations as well as for accountability.

Enterprises

The naming of enterprises can be a limiting factor of the network of enterprises (Cairns, 2023). My early use of the tool revealed that some participants wanted to break down enterprises into smaller specialisms, such as breaking their art practice enterprises into engagement with disciplines such as textiles and pottery, to further communicate their individuality (Cairns, 2023). However, in the use of network of enterprises, we see a turn towards sub-identities being clustered together (Schutz et al., 2020). As individuals take control of their networks of enterprises this naming protocol is possible, allowing the individual understudy the freedom to name their own enterprises. However, it will be necessary for individuals to consider if all their specialisms are main lines or if the overarching term is better placed to communicate involvement across the discipline. Naming enterprises is also limiting in terms of linguistic issues and standardisation of language used across networks of enterprises for different individuals. The case of Wallis shows this (Daichendt, 2011), while Wallis named himself an *artist-educator*, this is now often replaced with artist-teacher (Daichendt, 2009a, 2009b, 2010, 2011), which might raise questions about if both terms mean the same thing. However, networks of enterprises are focused on the individual, so it could be possible that the language used to name enterprises does not need to be universal and can instead be a personal choice.

The evolving milieu

Gruber's (1981) use of the network of enterprises drew some criticism from psychologist Mihaly Csikszentmihalyi (1988), who believed that creativity manifests in milieus or communities. Csikszentmihalyi felt Gruber focused too much on the individual understudy while neglecting the evolving community they operated in. This might be true; however, accompanying narrative accounts may be best placed here to tackle this issue (Wallace and Gruber, 1989). There is no clear way to document milieus, or how they change, within a network of enterprises. Wallace and Gruber (1989) give some attention to community, and there is a clear assumption of participation in communities connected to your enterprises from their perspective. The theme of community is implicit in identity, and wider work, such as Wenger et al's (2002), perhaps foregrounds this most eloquently and provides a natural assumption that identity is connected to community.

CONCLUSION

This chapter has outlined the network of enterprises as a tool used to chart and track involvement in different enterprises over time, with the purpose of providing a simplified overview of an individual's engagement in different enterprises and focus on goal achievement (Gruber and Wallace, 1999). Case studies of early use of the network of enterprises by Wallace and Gruber (1989) and Daichendt (2011) have shown how the tool has been used posthumously to document the lives of creative people and how they reached goals in different, but connected areas of their professional lives. Limitations of the network of enterprises were discussed, including the use of the tool and its indented audience, capturing identity flux and goals, and issues with linguistics and community. Ways of overcoming limitations were also shared, including the move from the network of enterprises being a case study tool to being a person-centred one that individuals can engage with, and importantly, it has been seen how these changes do not change the essence of the tool.

REFERENCES

Cairns, A. (2023) *Interrogating artist-teacher identity transformation in adult community learning.* Doctoral thesis, Norwich University of the Arts.

Csikszentmihalyi, M. (1988) 'Society, culture, and person: A systems view of creativity' in Sternberg, R. J. (ed.), *The nature of creativity: Contemporary psychological perspectives.* Cambridge: Cambridge University Press, pp. 325–339.

Daichendt, G. J. (2009a) 'George Wallis: The original artist-teacher', *Teaching Artist Journal,* 7(4), pp. 219–226. doi: 10.1080/15411790903158670.

Daichendt, G. J. (2009b) 'Redefining the artist-teacher', *Journal of Art Education,* 62(5), pp. 33–38. doi: 10.1080/00043125.2009.11519035.

Daichendt, G. J. (2010) *Artist-teacher: A philosophy for creating and teaching.* Bristol: Intellect.

Daichendt, G. J. (2011) 'The nineteenth-century artist-teacher: A case study of George Wallis and the creation of a new identity', *International Journal of Art and Design Education,* 30(1), pp. 71–80. doi: 10.1111/j.1476-8070.2011.01673.x.

Department for Education (DfE) (2018) *College staff survey 2018: Research report November 2018.* Available at: https://assets.publishing.service.gov.uk/government/uploads/system/uploads/attachment_data/file/920244/College_Staff_Survey_2018_main_report.pdf (Accessed 4 May 2024).

Education and Training Foundation (ETF) (2022) *Professional standards for teachers and trainers in the further education and training sector.* Available at: https://www.et-foundation.co.uk/wp-content/uploads/2022/04/PS-for-Teachers_Guide-to-Changes_Final.pdf (Accessed 28 May 2024).

Gruber, H. E. (1981) *Darwin on man: A psychological study of scientific creativity* (2nd ed.). Chicago: University of Chicago Press.

Gruber, H. E., and Wallace, D. B. (1999) 'The case study method and evolving systems approach for understanding unique creative people at work' in Sternberg, R. J. (ed.) *Handbook of creativity.* New York: Cambridge University Press, pp. 93–115.

Lave, J., and Wenger, E. (1991) *Situated learning: Legitimate peripheral participation.* Cambridge: Cambridge University Press.

McAdams, D. P. (1993) *The stories we live by: Personal myths and the making of the self.* New York: William Morrow & Co.

Schutz, P. A., Hong, J., and Francis, D. C. (2020) *Teachers' goals, beliefs, emotions, and identity development: Investigating complexities in the profession,* New York: Routledge.

Steadman, S. (2023) *Identity: Keywords in teacher education.* London: Bloomsbury Academic.

Wallace, D. B., and Gruber, H. E (1989) *Creative people at work: Twelve cognitive case studies*. New York: Oxford University Press.

Wenger, E. (2000) *Communities of practice: Learning meaning and identity*. Cambridge: University of Cambridge Press.

Wenger, E., McDermott, R. A., and Snyder, W. (2002) *Cultivating communities of practice: A guide to managing knowledge*. Boston: Harvard Business School Press.

CHAPTER THREE

How to use a network of enterprises

> **VIGNETTE: I'M A...**
>
> I am an artist. It is 2013, and I am standing in front of my artwork in an art gallery. I am a teacher. It is 2017, and I have a classroom and a whiteboard, the kind of board with the dry wipe whiteboard pens. I am a student. It is 2018, and each time I complete a course, I find myself applying for another. I am a researcher. It is 2020, and I sit at my laptop or with a book open, sometimes both at the same time. I am an author. It is 2024, and this is a surprising turn of events.
>
> Cairns, A. (2024) I'm a... Unpublished vignette.

This chapter outlines a step-by-step guide on creating and using a network of enterprises.

NAME YOUR ENTERPRISES

The first step in creating your network of enterprises is to name your enterprises. This tool is ideal for those with multifaceted identities. Hence, a network of enterprises is most beneficial for those who have or have had two or more enterprises across their professional career. There are several ways to capture your enterprise before you commit them to the tool, which will be explored next.

Identifying enterprises

In this chapter I have outlined five ways of identifying enterprises: inventory, audit, mapping, timeline, and seeking. These ways of identifying enterprises can be used on their own or in partnership with each other. The purpose of each is to help you identify your many enterprises over the span of your professional career. The use and difference of each identifying enterprises techniques is outlined below with a short description and an example of how I have used them. As you read the examples note how some of my answers to each prompt differ.

Enterprise inventory: This is a simple but effective technique that requires you to create a list of your various roles, past and present. At this stage it is also useful if you make a note of the dates each enterprise ran from and to. Your CV might be a good place to start, if you are having difficulties recalling roles and dates. However, there may be other enterprises you wish to add that have not made it onto your CV, such as hobbies or previous career paths. At this point it is beneficial to list everything, as you can remove enterprises if you find they are not main lines and have no bearing on your professional identity or goals.

When using the enterprise inventory, I relied on my CV to piece together my enterprise history, drawing from the education and career history sections. I took time to note the year(s) associated with each and roughly organised them chronologically. My identifying enterprises list can be viewed below:

Student (2012–2018, 2020–2023);
Artist (2012–presnt);
Gallery assistant (2013–2016);
Bartender (2017);
Art Teacher (2017–present);
Peer leader (2018–2020);
Facilitator (2018–present);
Researcher (2020–present);
Research assistant (2022–2023).

Enterprise audit: To discover your current enterprise(s) keep a time log for a week or a month to track how you spend your time and which enterprises you engage with. This method is only useful for current and ongoing enterprise and will not help you identify past enterprises. If you work in a more ad hoc way, you may want a longer auditing period.

When engaging with the enterprise audit my first consideration is how often I engage in each of my enterprises. I engage in some enterprises weekly;

however, I engage with others fortnightly or even monthly. To help ensure that I did not miss any enterprises I decided to audit a month. To do this I went over my calendar for January 2024 and noted every enterprise I came across. For example, when I saw teaching commitment written down, I knew I had engaged in my 'art teacher' enterprise; the other enterprises i engaged in are listed below.

> Art teacher;
> Mentor;
> Facilitator;
> Researcher;
> Artist.

You have the possibility to extend your use of the enterprise audit to help you start considering the time significance of each enterprise. To do this, note how often you engage in each enterprise you note down. See my worked example below for one week in January 2024 (Figure 3.1).

Weekday	Enterprise
Monday 8th	Facilitator Art teacher Artist Mentor
Tuesday 9th	Art teacher Researcher
Wednesday 10th	Mentor Facilitator Researcher
Thursday 11th	Mentor Researcher Facilitator Artist
Friday 12th	Researcher Art teacher
Saturday 13th	Artist Researcher
Sunday 14th	Artist Researcher Art teacher

FIGURE 3.1 My enterprise audit example.

Enterprise mapping: Use visual mapping with yourself at the centre and create branches for each enterprise. Enterprise mapping is particularly useful for those who enjoy working more visually. Within your map, you can start to document the dates each enterprise ran from and to, initial feelings on how significant each might be to you, and you can start to explore connections between your enterprises and current professional identity. Additionally, you might use the map to show relationships between enterprises, which may help you recognise which enterprises hold the most significance to your current professional identity.

I created my map digitally, but you can use pen and paper if you prefer. When creating my map, I was more focused on the relationships between my enterprises than with the previous techniques. In connecting these, I was able to recall enterprises that overlapped (Figure 3.2). This use of mapping helped me to identify enterprises that felt more significant, as I found the more the enterprises connected with other enterprises, the more significant it tended to be, While those with fewer connections felt less significant to my current professional identity.

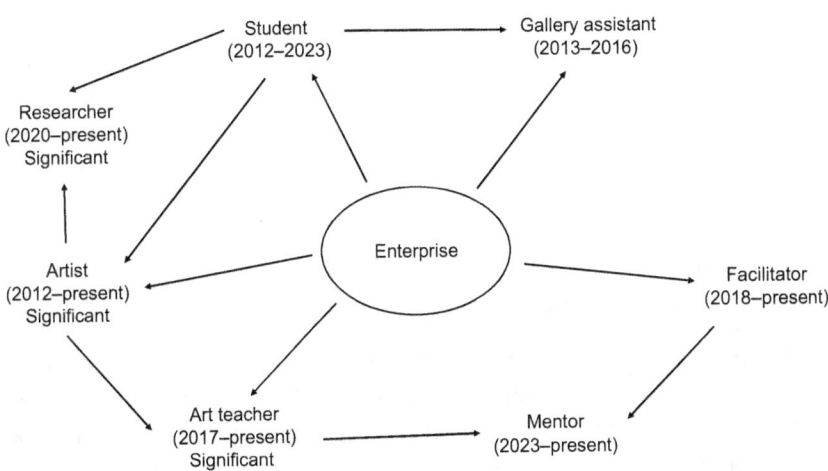

FIGURE 3.2 My enterprise mapping example.

Enterprise timeline: The enterprise timeline is a more structured system for recalling enterprises overtime and these can be most beneficial for those with long-spanning professional careers. Start your timeline with the year you began engaging in your professional career, this might be when you were in education, or once you joined the workforce and then move forward year-by-year until you reach the present day. This technique works on the notion of chronological organisation, where the use of sequencing can be beneficial for information recall. The completed timeline will become a useful quick reference guide when you come to put your network of enterprises together and make clear where enterprises continue across years or where they make fleeting appearances in your professional life.

My timeline runs from the start of my degree in fine art to today (Figure 3.3). When putting the timeline together I focused first on the key enterprise of each year and then reflected to see if other enterprises came to mind. For example, I knew that when I was completing my BA I also worked as a gallery assistant. This made the placement of the latter enterprise easier by association.

Year	Enterprises
2013-2016	Student Artist Gallery Assistant
2017	Student Artist Teacher
2018	Student Artist Teacher Facilitator
2019-2020	Artist Teacher Facilitator
2020-2023	Artist Teacher Facilitator Student Researcher
2024	Artist Teacher Facilitator Researcher

FIGURE 3.3 My enterprise timeline example.

Enterprise seeking: If you are struggling to identify your enterprises, ask colleagues, family, or friends which enterprises they associate with you. External perspectives may offer you valuable insights into your enterprises and uncover areas you have overlooked.

It was only when I engaged in enterprise seeking that my overlooked enterprises were revealed to me:

> Ice skater;
> Content creator.

I had not considered these two enterprises in the inventory, audit, or mapping techniques. While the ice skater identity is perhaps a little too far removed as an enterprise from my professional identity to feature on my network of enterprises, it does highlight my engagement in the student enterprise and the significance of being a lifelong learner to me. The content creator, however, was an overlooked enterprise on my part. On reflection, this is an enterprise I have significant involvement in and one that crosses over many of my other enterprises.

Naming your enterprises prompt questions

- *What role(s) do I carry out?*
- *What hobbies and activities do I engage in?*

HOW TO USE A NETWORK OF ENTERPRISES

- *What are my official job titles?*
- *What am I involved in that takes up space in my professional life?*

PICK A TIMEFRAME

The network of enterprises replies upon a personally set timeframe. Your timeframe should take you from the start of your professional career to the present day. I have identified three timeframe options: year blocks, years, and months. Ultimately, there is no one-size-fits-all timeframe, and you may find it helpful to experiment with different timeframes. By testing a few out, you will be better able to adjust your network of enterprises to ensure that it is as efficient as possible for you.

Timeframes

Year blocks: If you have had a long career you may want to work in block of time such as three, five, or ten years. The benefit of working in this way is that your network of enterprises remains a manageable size. However, you might find it difficult to judge the significance of each enterprise over large time blocks, as it might be the case that your engagement in each enterprise was different every year, of any given time block. Here is it important to work with averaging involvement out to ensure that your network of enterprise is accurate.

In Figure 3.4, I have used three-year time blocks; this is due to the length of my professional career. When tracking each enterprise over time I am considering each of the three years, for example, in 2012, I had not started to consider art as an enterprise yet, which brought the significance of art down to minimal in the 2012–2014 timeframe.

Month	Art	Teaching
2012-2014		
2015-2017		
2016-2018		
2019-2021		
2022-2024		

FIGURE 3.4 My network of enterprises three-year block example.

Years: Yearly time intervals work well for most people and allow for a more in-depth look at enterprises over time than year blocks. Yearly intervals still require you to average out involvement in each enterprise over a year and for some this might not be nuanced enough. However, it has the benefit of giving a good overview of your professional career.

In my experience, year intervals work well as it allowed me to look back at a glance. Plotting the significance of each enterprise took a little consideration as I worked out the average significance of each enterprise in each year (Figure 3.5).

Year	Art	Teaching
2014		
2015		
2016		
2017		
2018		
2019		
2020		
2021		
2022		
2023		
2024		

FIGURE 3.5 My yearly network of enterprise example.

Months: If you are at the start of your professional career, you may find smaller increments of time more beneficial, such as monthly blocks. Additionally, you might find monthly intervals useful if you find it difficult to average out yearly significance and involvement. The benefit of this timeframe is that it allows for a nuanced look back and is better able to show the flux of enterprises over time. The drawback is that if you plot every month of every year of your professional career your network of enterprises will become incredibly long. Additionally, when looking further back it may be difficult to recall involvement for each month, due to this, it is best used for most recent year(s).

My monthly network of enterprises documents the ebbs and flows of my professional career easily (Figure 3.6). The plotting of significance starts to reveal patterns and highlight how enterprises interact with one another. The structure of teaching becomes clear, with holidays coinciding with the significance of teaching lessening and art becoming more significant.

Month (2024)	Art	Teaching
January		
February		
March		
April		
May		
June		
July		
August		
September		
October		
November		
December		

FIGURE 3.6 My monthly network of enterprise example.

Pick a timeframe prompt questions

- *When did my professional career begin?*
- *Have I had more than one professional career?*
- *How long was I engaged in formal education for?*
- *Are there any gaps in my career history?*

Deep dive

It is also possible to use the network of enterprises to deep dive into any period of your professional career. For this, regardless of the longevity of your professional career, the monthly network of enterprises is most appropriate. Deep dives are most effective when looking at the current year or back on the previous year. You may find it beneficial to Complete each month of your network of enterprises on the last day of the month, as this takes away the need to recall this information at the end of the year, resulting in a more accurate representation of each enterprise.

ASSESS THE SIGNIFICANCE OF INVOLVEMENT

To assess the significance of involvement of each of your enterprises you will first need to set your own criteria for what lens you will look at this through. Within the network of enterprises, you may decide to consider involvement through the lens of time or personal change or several other lenses outlined below. It is important to pick a lens before committing to creating a network of enterprises to ensure that you are reflecting on each enterprise in the same way and judging each by the same criteria as this will ensure a level of consistency throughout your network of enterprises. You may find that each lens creates a different network of enterprises despite the enterprises remaining the same; this is due to the differing criteria of each lens. For example, if I looked at teaching through the lens of time it may appear more significant than it would if it was looked at through the lens of passion (Figure 3.7).

Network of enterprises lenses

In the original works by Wallace and Gruber (1989) and Daichendt's (2009) work with George Wallace it is not stated which lens is used to create the network of enterprises. This is limiting because, as with my example in 3.7, different lenses will impact the network of enterprises. It is therefore important to consider which aligns most with your goals. The use of a lens will provide you with focus and direction, better enabling you to make sense of your enterprises. Additionally, each lens will shape how you interpret and visualise each enterprise.

EXPLORING YOUR FURTHER EDUCATION TEACHER IDENTITY

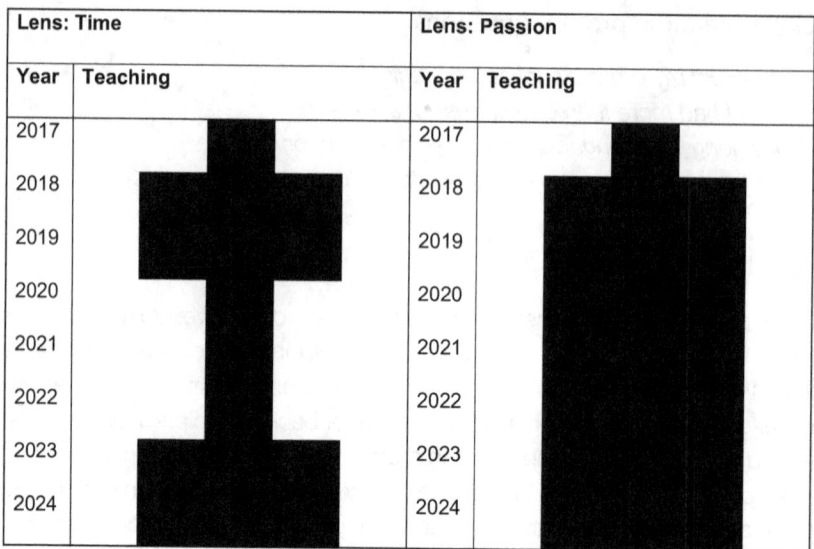

FIGURE 3.7 My time and passion lens network of enterprise examples.

Lenses

I have identified five lenses: time, remuneration, passion, personal, and professional. These lenses provide five nuanced frameworks for viewing your enterprises. The use and difference of each is outlined below with a short description of the lens and an example of how I have applied it to my own enterprises. Each worked example is accompanied by a snippet of what my network of enterprises might look like.

Time: With this lens, you will consider your enterprises by how much time they take up in any given period, as outlined on your network of enterprises. Something that takes up a lot of your time, such as full-time teaching would be charted as more significant than a hobby related to your vocation, which you only spend a limited amount of time on. With this lens, you can document how this involvement changes over time as you look back on your professional career.

When I use this lens to reflect on the enterprises of art and teaching, I note that during 2017–2018 when I was completing my MA in fine art, art took up a

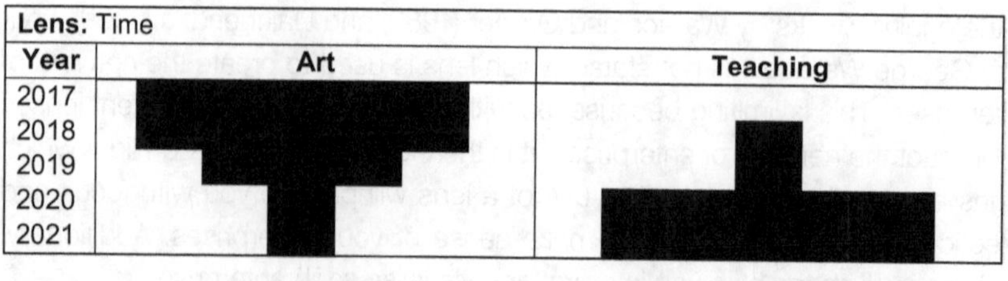

FIGURE 3.8 My time lens network of enterprise example.

lot of my time, while teaching was non-existent in 2017, as I was yet to enter the profession. As the years go on there is a clear relationship between the significance of art and teaching in my life (Figure 3.8).

Remuneration: This lens is concerned with the money you receive from each enterprise you participate in. When using the remuneration lens, you will scale enterprises on how much income they generate in any given period, as outlined on your network of enterprises. You may find that as your career progresses, different enterprises emerge as the most lucrative.

When using the remuneration lens, I can reflect on each enterprise in relation to money gained from them. The significance of remuneration to my art enterprise is nominal while I enjoy making and exhibiting artwork as an artist; I have never actively tried to sell my work. In contrast, I can reflect on the growing significance of remuneration to my teacher enterprise (Figure 3.9).

Lens: Remuneration		
Year	Art	Teaching
2017		
2018		
2019		
2020		

FIGURE 3.9 My remuneration lens network of enterprises example.

Passion: The passion lens is concerned with the amount of joy and fulfilment each of your enterprises brings you in any given period, as outlined on your network of enterprises. The stronger the sense of passion, the more significant the enterprise. You might find that your passion for an enterprise does not wane over time or that what you are passionate about changes as your career progresses.

When using the passion lens, I reflect on each enterprise to gauge how excited I am about it. The more joy it brings, the more significant it is. While I may have lost time for art, I have not lost my passion for it. My passion for teaching is also significant. However, there is a clear margin between the two, with art being my first love (Figure 3.10).

Lens: Passion		
Year	Art	Teaching
2021		
2022		
2023		
2024		

FIGURE 3.10 My passion lens network of enterprises example.

Personal: The personal lens allows you to consider how you rate each enterprise in a more emotional way, allowing you to evaluate the emotional impact each enterprise has on you. With this lens, enterprises can be considered concerning how big or small they feel to you, how they relate to your personal development in terms of lessons learned or skills gained, and how well each enterprise aligns with your own values and beliefs.

When using a personal lens, I am engaging in a reasoning process that is guided by my gut instinct (Figure 3.11). I am weighing up how each enterprise sits with me, and in this process, I find that art is more significant to me than teaching. Art feels more personal, and it is self-directed and completed in my own time and environment. Teaching is still very much there and has significance; however, it does not feel as significant through the personal lens. Interestingly, while I found consistency amongst my art and teaching enterprises, I found the significance of research changed with this lens. When reflecting with the personal lens I can reason that this is because research came to be a very personal activity for me due to my subject area.

Lens: Personal			
Year	Art	Teaching	Research
2021			
2022			
2023			
2024			

FIGURE 3.11 My personal lens network of enterprises example.

Professional: The professional lens allows you to consider the significance of enterprises on your professional identity. Some enterprises will have a more significant bearing on your current professional identity than others. You may find that involvement in early enterprises has informed your career path.

When using the professional lens, it is clear to see that undertaking a degree in fine art had a hugely significant impact on my becoming an artist-teacher. Without this initial training, I simply would not have started teaching. In contrast, I can look back on my time as a gallery assistant and see that it had little significance in comparison to my fine art degree, despite being a role connected to art, I have not worked in a gallery since (Figure 3.12).

Lens: Professional		
Year	BA Fine Art	Gallery Assistant
2013		
2014		
2015		
2016		

FIGURE 3.12 My professional lens network of enterprises example.

Scaling

The network of enterprises required you to assess your involvement in each enterprise listed. The scaling exercise, shared next, is at the heart of any network of enterprises and is reliant on your ability to undertake a self-assessment. Once complete the use of scaling provides a snapshot of your subjective evaluations on enterprises engaged with. Daichendt (2009) used a scaling system with three options:

- Significant involvement;
- Involvement and;
- Minor to no involvement.

This type of qualitative scaling will allow you to self-assess your involvement and its significance ranging from high to none. Each option is accompanied by a visual representation, depicted in a key within the network of enterprises (Figure 3.13).

Significant involvement	Involvement	Minor to no involvement

FIGURE 3.13 Network of enterprises three-tiered key.

The act of scaling your involvement allows you to communicate clearly your involvement in each enterprise, providing you with a nuanced evaluation of your professional career. When putting together your network of enterprises you will be required to make a judgement of your involvement for each enterprise for each block of time you are reporting. For example, you might find that before you entered teaching your involvement here was minor, as you moved into part-time teaching you would have seen your involvement increase and as you take on a full-time teaching position your involvement in teaching becomes significant. Your involvement in enterprises is always in flux, and a career break from teaching might see the significance of this enterprise return to minor (Figure 3.14).

You may find that these three scaling options do not offer you enough variation and you might choose to use another scale. You will need to ensure that your choice of descriptive language is appropriate, represents differing levels of significance of involvement, and can be applied to evaluating significance of involvement in enterprises.

You may find that a five-point scale is more appropriate for your needs and better allows you to assess the significance of each enterprise in your life. Whether using the three-point scale or five-point scale the purpose of scaling is to help you gauge the significance of enterprises over time.

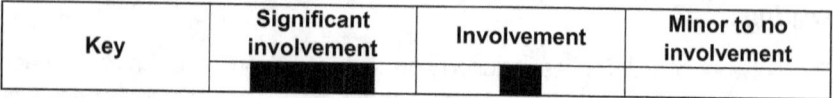

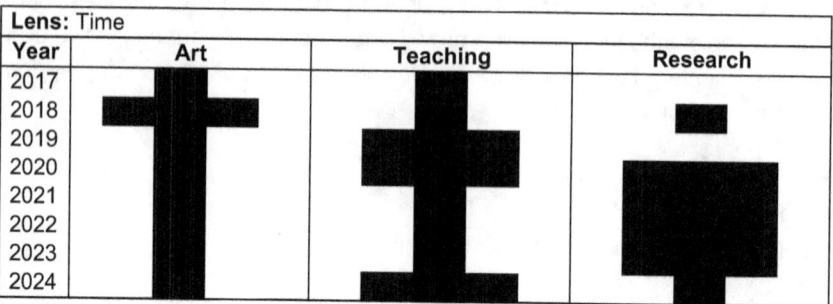

FIGURE 3.14 My network of enterprises three-tiered example.

Option one:

- Very significant;
- Significant;
- Moderately significant;
- Slightly significant;
- Non-significant.

Option two:

- Very involved;
- Somewhat involved;
- Involved;
- Neutral;
- Not involved at all.

The terms in Figure 3.15 are understood as follows. A very significant enterprise is of high importance in your life, and this enterprise impacts and influences all areas of your life. A significant enterprise is important and engagement in it is meaningful, and again it is likely to impact and influence your life. Moderately significant enterprises hold some importance and are likely to still feature heavily in your life. Enterprises that are slightly significant are not a major consideration in your life but are still noticeable, but they hold less importance to you and have less of an impact on your life. Non-significant enterprises are not active, and they do not influence your life or hold any notable importance nor impact your life.

Very significant	Significant	Moderately significant	Slightly significant	Non-significant

FIGURE 3.15 Network of enterprises five-tiered key.

Once you have decided on an appropriate scaling system, return to your identified enterprises and assign the significance of involvement to each across each year, using your chosen lens. You may find it easier to start with the current year and work backwards, as your current enterprise and involvement in them today will have been shaped by the past. By starting with the current year, you can use recent experiences to provide context for previous years and you will be able to better interpret past enterprises and make better sense of your professional career. Additionally, by starting from your current enterprises, you are more likely to be able to retrospectively select the most salient previous enterprises to include within your network of enterprises as main lines, giving the task focus and ensuring that it is a meaningful undertaking.

In this activity, it is important to ensure that you have selected the most relevant scaling term. At this stage you might find it useful to make some brief notes exploring the reasons why an enterprise is very significant, significant, moderately significant, slightly significant, or non-significant. You can use the questions below to prompt your thinking.

Assessing the significance of involvement prompt questions

- *Is enterprise one as significant as enterprises two, three, and four?*
- *If you had to order your enterprises which is most significant and which is least significant?*
- *Can you have two very significant enterprises in the same year?*
- *If enterprise one was significant this year, how significant was it last year/ten years ago?*
- *What factors have influenced enterprise three being moderately significant?*

FUTURE PLANNING

Networks of enterprises were developed with goal achievement in mind (Wallace and Gruber, 1989); by using your network of enterprise to look forward you will be better equipped to reach your goals. This stage requires you to know what your professional goals are. However, if you are unsure you can begin by surveying your completed network of enterprise and reflecting on whether you are happy with where you are or if you want things to change (Figure 3.16). You should consider this question through the same lens that you used to create your network of enterprise.

EXPLORING YOUR FURTHER EDUCATION TEACHER IDENTITY

Key	Significant involvement	Involvement	Minor to no involvement
	■	■	

Lens: Year	Art	Teaching	Research	Mentoring	Facilitating
2023	■	■	■	■	■

FIGURE 3.16 My future planning network of enterprises example.

If your goals for each enterprise are unaligned with their current significance for a year, use the tool to document the change you would like to see by looking one to five years ahead. Remember to check in with your network of enterprises as time passes to judge your level of involvement in each enterprise and to check your progress. Your network of enterprises can be used in decision-making processes about the future of your professional career and can be used as a tool to help you uncover insights into your perception of what your future may look like. The network of enterprises encourages the use of prioritising, as you start to scale the enterprise you hope to continue to be involved in; in future years, keep in mind that some enterprises will need to be more significant than others.

Goal setting

The scaling of each enterprise, according to a selected lens, should aid you in developing a more detailed action plan, strategy, or interventions to ensure you reach your intended goals. The network of enterprise is intended to help you focus on areas you wish to address. When setting goals using the network of enterprises try documenting future years in another colour to make differentiation between documented years and goal years clear.

In using the network of enterprises to set my own goals I have looked three years ahead. You may find the further forward you look, the more difficult it is to set goals. To help differentiate the past from the future I have set my goals in grey and kept my current involvement in black (Figure 3.17). The five enterprises that I chose to document are the ones that felt the most significant to my professional identity, my main lines. However, when outlining goals for the future I had to be realistic and realise that I could not have significant time involvement in all five. I can now use this as a template when scheduling these enterprises into my daily life and revisit the network of enterprises to see if I am on track to meet each goal.

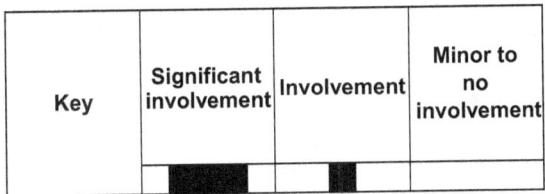

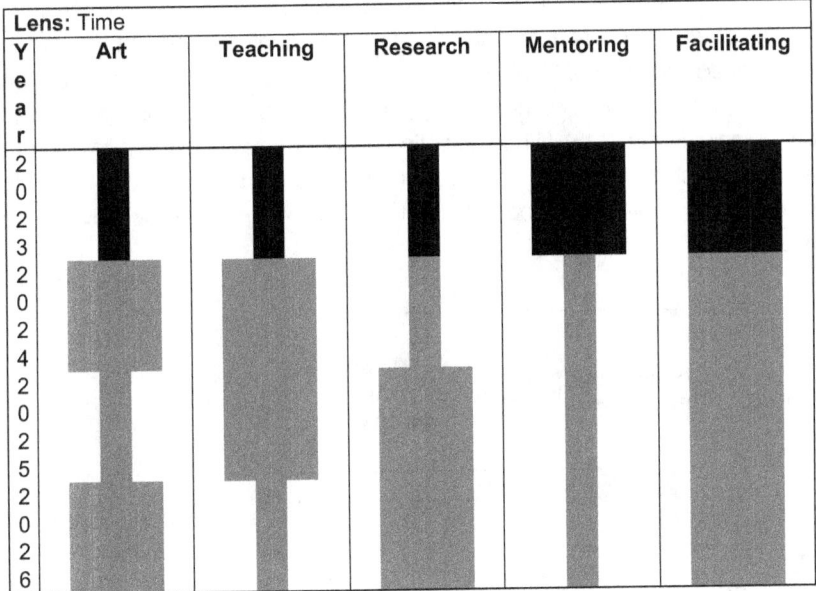

FIGURE 3.17 My goal setting network of enterprises example.

Future planning prompt questions

What is your goal in your professional career?
What are your aspirations for the next 3–5 years?
Do you anticipate any changes in the next 3–5 years in your professional life?

Revisiting

Use your network of enterprises to monitor your progress towards your goals and ensure that you schedule time to assess how well you are balancing each

EXPLORING YOUR FURTHER EDUCATION TEACHER IDENTITY

enterprise by deciding how often you will revisit the tool. Mark onto your network of enterprises any changes to goals as well as where goals have been met. You may find that goals for each enterprise change, particularly when looking five years ahead. Your network of enterprises is yours to adjust, ensure you take ownership and adjust it if your needs, circumstances, or priorities change. As you re-engage with the network of enterprises use colour to highlight if the goal has been achieved. If the goal has been achieved the significance will go from grey to black. If you have not achieved the goal, grey will still be visible. This colour coding will give you a quick way of assessing and reading your network of enterprises.

Within my network of enterprises, you can see if the time goals for teaching, mentoring, and facilitating were met, as the involvement for these in 2024 is showing as a solid back column. In contrast, you can see that the time goal for art was not met, I had planned for 'significant involvement' (grey) but only reached 'involvement' (black). Similarly, I did not reach my time goal for research, aiming for 'involvement '(grey), I ended up having 'significant involvement' (black) (Figure 3.18). When reflecting on this, I can conclude that I did not spend as much time on art, as I spent more time than planned on research, this realisation provides a good time to stop and consider my next move going forward.

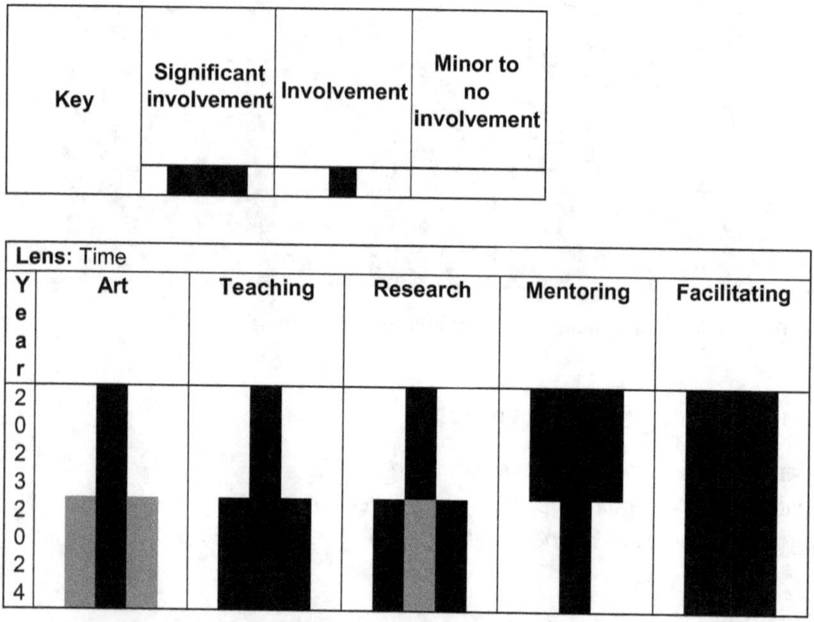

Key	Significant involvement	Involvement	Minor to no involvement
	■	■	

Lens: Time					
Year	Art	Teaching	Research	Mentoring	Facilitating
2023 2024					

FIGURE 3.18 My revisiting network of enterprises example.

HOW TO USE A NETWORK OF ENTERPRISES

Revisiting prompt questions

Have you met your goals?
If you have not met your goals, do you need to make a change?
Have your goals changed since you set them?

Create your network or enterprises prompt questions

Are all these enterprises necessary?
Have I missed out a pertinent enterprise?
Is the timeframe working?
Have I chosen the most appropriate scale?
Have I balanced out the significance of involvement for each?

TRY THIS! CREATE YOUR NETWORK OF ENTERPRISES

You are now ready to create your own network of enterprises, by bringing together your list of enterprises, timeframe, your chosen lens, and scale. Work in a basic table formation created digitally or drawn by hand. It is worth noting that digital networks of enterprises have the benefit of being easily edited. Plot your time scale down the left-hand side of the network of enterprises and list your enterprises across the top of your page. Make a note of the lens you have used as this will be a useful reminder when revisiting the network of enterprises to check on your progress. Work systematically to apply your involvement scale. As you put your network of enterprises together you may find that you edit your list of enterprises and only include the ones most pertinent to your professional identity and goals.

When putting my final network of enterprises together I decided to include six enterprises: art, teaching, research, mentoring, facilitating, and being a student, as these all felt like significant parts of my professional identity (Figure 3.19). The time scale starts the year after I finished my BA in fine art, as before then I did not have much involvement in any of these most pertinent enterprises. I chose the time lens as I find time to be my biggest stumbling block and would be most useful to track over time and have used a three-tiered scale for simplicity.

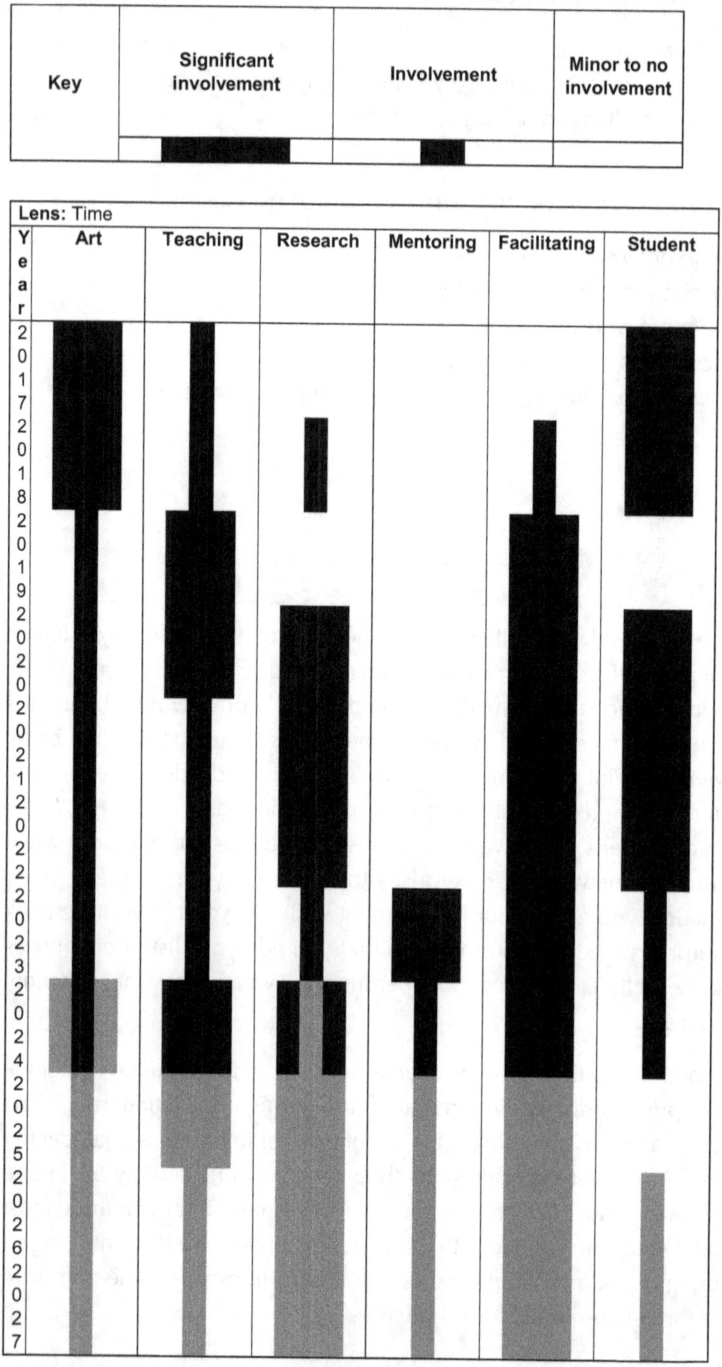

EXPLORING YOUR FURTHER EDUCATION TEACHER IDENTITY

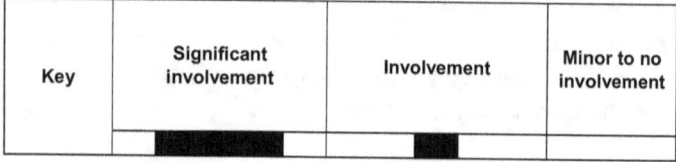

FIGURE 3.19 My completed network of enterprises example.

REFERENCES

Daichendt, G. J. (2009) 'George Wallis: The original artist-teacher', *Teaching Artist Journal*, 7(4), pp. 219–226. doi: 10.1080/15411790903158670.

Wallace, D. B., and Gruber, H. E. (1989) *Creative people at work: Twelve cognitive case studies.* New York: Oxford University Press.

CHAPTER FOUR

From use to insight
FE teacher and trainers' reflections on the network of enterprises

> **VIGNETTE: I'M HERE AND I'M ME**
>
> How do you move out of the way of a shadow? More light is needed directly overhead. Each time I sidestep, my shadow comes too. If I shed some light on other FE teacher and trainer's thoughts, maybe my shadow might fade away.
> Cairns, A. (2022) I'm here and I'm me. Unpublished vignette.

INTRODUCTION

In this chapter, reflections from FE teachers and trainers are shared. The purpose of this chapter is to highlight the use of the network of enterprise by practitioners in the sector. Their experience is intended to help you better understand and negotiate your use of the tool and the techniques used within it. For each technique, the benefits, limitations, ease of use, and impact on professional identity are explored. The FE teachers and trainers drawn upon in this chapter were recruited to take part via an online open call across social media platforms, and their participation was voluntary. Each FE teacher and trainer quoted in this chapter has given permission for their experiences, and their names to be shared to help situate the tool in real life.

Before we begin, let me introduce you to eight of the FE teachers and trainers who have been testing the network of enterprises: Audrey Fairgrieve, Beth Curtis, Dr Gary Husband, Elizabeth Draper, Heather Booth-Martin, Jason Boucher, Kerry E Heathcote, and Toby Doncaster.

DOI: 10.4324/9781003497813-6

FROM USE TO INSIGHT

NAMING YOUR ENTERPRISES

The FE teachers and trainers who engaged with the network of enterprises were introduced to this stage of the tool, naming your enterprise, as having the aim of helping you compile all your enterprises in one place. The FE teachers and trainers were introduced to the five different techniques outlined in this book to name enterprises: inventory, audit; mapping; timeline; and seeking. FE teachers and trainers were initially asked to pick one technique, but many selected two or three that they felt worked well together to help them successfully name all their enterprises, while Heather suggested that she could see purpose in all the presented techniques.

Enterprise inventory

The enterprise inventory was introduced as a simple list of enterprises that could be recall in the moment of the task. The extract below outlines Audrey's interaction with this technique.

> The inventory...I think [its] quite concrete and but also quite flexible.
> - Audrey

Audery found that the enterprise inventory provided structure to her thinking but that its flexibility allowed her to adapt this stage to her own needs and preferences in working through the process of naming enterprises. This allowed her a sense of ownership and control over the process, leading to a deeper and more honest network of enterprises. Limitations highlighted include the technique being too narrow, putting you at risk of accidently missing enterprises. However, multiple ways of naming enterprises can be used to overcome this.

> [The inventory is] potentially easy to start off with, but it might become more difficult when you start to think about things that you do and connections that you make and how they fit in.
> - Audrey

Audrey found the enterprise inventory initially easy to handle, and her experience suggested the technique and the initial steps of this stage are user-friendly and straightforward. Ease of entry can encourage engagement with the tool. However, Audrey found that further engagement with this technique became more complex and further her thinking developed. This complexity arises from reflecting on enterprises and integrating these insights into the inventory, which indicates that the inventory encourages deep, meaningful engagement, pushing users to think critically about their enterprises. Engagement in this technique made FE teachers and trainers consider what their professional identity might or might not be and helped them to view professional identity as flexible.

Enterprise audit

The enterprise audit was introduced as a technique that asks you to look back at your diary for the last month/year and note which enterprises you engaged with. The extract below outlines Heather's interaction with this technique.

> I think benefit-wise, the first that comes to my mind is…time management [and] listing all the things you do.
>
> - Heather

Heather's experience of enterprise auditing highlights significant benefits of the technique. For Heather, the act of listing all her enterprises provides her with a clear overview that she may not have typically considered. This snapshot allowed for a more holistic understanding of her responsibilities and workload. Heather suggested that a limitation might be that an audit does not capture all enterprises, as not everything, such as engagement with social media, will be captured in diaries. Heather felt the audit initially seemed an easy task, albeit one that might require time to be completed comprehensively.

> I think in the world of education, we hold many hats… I think we have multiple identities.
>
> - Heather

A comprehensive enterprise list allowed Heather to identify redundant or low-value enterprises and enhanced her awareness of her professional identity. Overall, it was felt by FE teachers and trainers that enterprise auditing had a positive impact on their professional identities, as the process encouraged reflection and fostered a mindset geared towards continuing professional development.

Enterprise mapping

Enterprise mapping was introduced as a technique for creating a visual map with your professional self in the middle and your enterprises coming off from this central anchor, allowing you to visualise which enterprise relates to which. The extract below outlines Kerry's interaction with this technique.

> The benefit [of mapping] is actually that [its] quite motivational… when I'm feeling a bit jaded, if I look at it, I think actually I do quite a lot… I feel quite proud that I'm quite enterprising.
>
> - Kerry

Kerry found that her engagement in enterprise mapping had a motivational impact and that revisiting the finished map served as a powerful reminder of her accomplishments. For Kerry, the network of enterprises became a tool for positive self-assessment with the visual depiction reinforcing Kerry's understanding of her enterprising spirit and providing her with a renewed sense of professional identity.

Kerry felt that a limitation of enterprise mapping could be the overwhelming nature of seeing how many enterprises you are engaged in. However, overall, Kerry felt the benefits outweigh the negatives, as it allowed her to reflect on everything she had achieved and be proud that she had not given up. Kerry found completing enterprise mapping easy but noted it took some time to complete a comprehensive map. Kerry additionally engaged in aspects of enterprise auditing to help ensure she had named all her enterprises.

> [It] made me consider my professional identity... I've deliberately got involved in more enterprises outside of work ... and I hadn't reflected on it like that before.
>
> - Kerry

Enterprise mapping made Kerry consider her professional identity in terms of both paid work and other enterprises, which allowed Kerry to shift her perception of her professional identity. Enterprise mapping also allowed for deep reflection and a newfound awareness of enterprises. For Kerry this highlighted how her extra efforts and broader engagement contributed to her overall professional identity and CPD activities.

Enterprise timeline

The enterprise timeline was introduced as being similar to the enterprise inventory technique but organised chronologically. The extract below outlines Elizabeth and Gary's experiences with the technique.

> [It] shows the ways I have developed and the connections I've made and the way I've grown within education, further education and my discipline.
>
> - Elizabeth

Elizabeth's engagement in the enterprise timeline allowed her to reflect on her journey of personal and professional growth through her involvement in enterprises overtime. Elizabeth indicated that use of the technique highlighted how time spent in different enterprises contributed to her overall maturation and professional identity formation. Elizabeth found that through this technique she could better understand how she had navigated challenges and leveraged opportunities for self-improvement. The enterprise timeline had a focus on connections for Elizabeth, as the enterprise timeline is organised chronologically, it was easy for her to see how enterprises overlapped or continued from one another. However, Elizabeth did find one limitation of the tool, sharing that the use of the term enterprises was unfamiliar and therefore made naming her enterprises difficult, as she had to gain an understanding of what an enterprise is or could be first.

> It's clear, it provides a little bit of clarity... I'm constantly asked, every time I go to a different meeting... 'can you tell us about yourself?'... having some sort of clarity and logical way of approaching that's really good, but also there's an element there about trajectory, where you are going next and how have some things fallen away.
>
> - Gary

Gary valued the enterprise timeline for its clarity and structured approach and felt that the technique would aid in articulating his experiences and background effectively to others. The clear and logical timeline produced helped Gary to maintain consistency in his narrative across various contexts and ensured a coherent story of experiences of enterprises, including those that have become less relevant or have changed over time. Gary found that the technique effectively showed not only where he has been but also where he is headed.

Enterprise seeking

Enterprise seeking was introduced as a technique that encourages you to ask others which enterprises they associate with you. The extract below outlines Toby's experiences of the technique.

> I'm quite an introvert, so I've never, I would never have thought of asking someone else.
>
> - Toby

For Toby, enterprise seeking opened an otherwise missed opportunities to engage with others about his professional identity. Toby shared that before encountering this technique he had not considered asking others about his enterprises. Toby's experience sheds light on the internal barriers that may be encounter when enterprise seeking. While the idea of reaching out to others about enterprises might feel uncomfortable, this technique made Toby think about who he might ask and suggested using the tool with a few trusted people. Other FE teacher and trainers who have used the tool suggested they would prefer to use it independently, without the involvement of others.

PICKING A TIME FRAME

Next, FE teachers and trainers were introduced to the timeframe element of the network of enterprises. It was outlined that selected timeframes should take you from the start of your professional career to the present day. The FE teachers and trainers were introduced to the three suggested timeframes: year blocks, years, and months.

Year blocks

Year blocks were introduced as best for those with long careers. It was suggested FE teachers and trainers might work in blocks of three, five, or ten years. The extract below outline Kerry's experiences of the technique. Kerry suggested she would use three-year blocks, as she felt this sat well with her career.

> I can see how far I've come actually from the girl… in the Wimpy serving who could only carry one plate at a time … [to] being somebody who's sitting here, hopefully just about to finally become a doctor… It gives… me a full picture of steps I've taken to be able to be sitting here today.
>
> - Kerry

For Kerry three-year blocks allowed her to illustrate her journey of enterprise engagement and professional identity development. Kerry liked that the chronological plotting of her career gave her a tangible representation of progression that might otherwise be overlooked. This technique helped to provide clarity and a sense of accomplishment, reinforcing the importance of self-awareness in professional development. Three-year blocks gave Kerry a sense of fulfilment and purpose and became a powerful tool for acknowledging growth.

Kerry did not feel there were any limitations to year blocks and found the technique very easy to engage with. She did, however, feel that shorter year blocks would be limiting and would not effectively capture who she is. Other FE teachers and trainers reported they would engage in longer year blocks (five-or-ten-years) due to longer careers.

Yearly

Yearly blocks were introduced as a good allrounder suitable for most FE teachers and trainers. The extract below outlines Gary's experiences of the technique.

> I think years is the most sensible one here… we're only going back 28, 27 years or something [so] it's not going to end up huge.
>
> - Gary

Gary's choice to plot his career year-by-year reflects his thoughtful consideration of both the comprehensiveness and manageability of the technique. Plotting his career yearly provided a clear and sequential narrative of his professional journey. Gary felt this technique was the most straightforward and provided a sufficiently detailed view of his enterprise progression without becoming unwieldy. Gary found this technique to be a practical approach to visualising engagement in enterprises, which facilitated easy identification of significant milestones, transitions, and patterns over time. Other FE teachers and trainers noted that their careers felt too long to document in this way. A limitation that arose was overlooking or forgetting enterprises that did not last a year.

Months

Month blocks were introduced as ideal for those at the start of their career or those who want to deep dive into the current year. The extract below outlines Heather's experiences of the technique.

> I could see trainee teachers doing a monthly [network of enterprises].
>
> - Heather

Heather highlighted how breaking down engagement in enterprises into monthly blocks may aid trainee teachers, as this would allow them to plot themselves regularly, foster continuous growth, and embed a sense of accountability. This accountability can lead to increased motivation and a proactive approach to learning, as monthly blocks allow the trainee teachers to focus without losing sight of their overarching goals, promoting a healthier work-life balance. Heather suggested monthly blocks can also serve as a platform for discussing progress with mentors or peers. Other FE teachers and trainers suggested that monthly blocks might be limiting for those with longer careers as you would need to be able to recall each month in close detail, which becomes more difficult as time passes.

ASSESSING THE SIGNIFICANCE OF ENTERPRISES

FE teachers and trainers were introduced to assessing the significance of involvement of each of your enterprises as a task that requires use of a lens. Lenses were introduced as ways of looking at enterprises and five lenses were introduced: time; remuneration; passion; personal; and professional. The extract below outlines Kerry, Audery, and Heather's experiences of assessing the significance of their enterprises.

> Whether or not [an enterprise is] significant chronologically or significant now is a philosophical question.
>
> - Kerry

Kerry's reflection on the tool questioned how significance is measured over time. Kerry outlined that the significance of enterprises can shift, and an enterprise deemed significant now may not have held the same value in the past, and vice versa. For Kerry, an important aspect of this process is that the enterprises she outlined carried a legacy and had a long-term impact on her professional identity. Kerry found the subjectivity of significance to be the main limitation and noted that enterprises could look differently through each lens and day-to-day.

> [Wanting more than one lens] is almost like muddying the waters, in terms of seeing those links between time or it could be passion and significance… I think it would be fairly easy if I'm aligning significance to one of the lenses. I think that would make things easier because you've got something [to] construct, to assess the significance against.
>
> - Audrey

Audrey commented on the use of multiple lenses. Several FE teachers and trainers who have engaged in the tool considered using two lenses, and it was suggested that some lenses might be linked, i.e. passion and professional, and that using two might offer a richer, more comprehensive understanding of enterprise significance. However, Audrey preferred a structured method where she assessed significance against a singular lens. She stated that multiple lenses complicated the assessment process, making it harder to draw definitive conclusions on each enterprise's significance as it may also introduce ambiguity. In contrast, she found that working with a singular lens added a level of clarity.

> I think I would have to think about things in more detail through the lenses. But I don't think that's a bad thing… it really makes you think [about] what's serving your purpose.
>
> - Heather

Heather found the task of assessing significance of enterprises through different lenses to be a slow but beneficial process and suggested that consideration of enterprises through each lens, individually, might be beneficial in gaining a more nuanced understanding of her professional identity. She found that the lenses encouraged deeper contemplation about what enterprises are truly serving her goals and recognised the evaluative nature of using these lenses.

Time

The time lens was introduced as assessing enterprise significance in terms of how much time you spend on each. FE teachers and trainers who have engaged with the tool found this lens straight forward to engage in. The extract below outlines Jason and Gary's experiences with this lens.

> How much time [do] I spend on an enterprise? Well, I've just written 3 words here; work, writing, [and] education. There may be a couple of others, but work is probably the one that takes too much time, writing too little and education not enough.
>
> - Jason

Jason uses the time lens to assess the significance of three enterprises – work, writing, and education – and his reflections are succinct yet insightful. Through this lens, Jason identified a potential imbalance where work dominates his daily schedule. For Jason, the network of enterprises was key in pinpointing his desire to engage more in certain enterprises, with the insufficient time spent on writing suggesting neglect of this important enterprise. With use of the tool and this lens, Jason could address this imbalance, helping him to achieve a more satisfying and well-rounded professional identity.

> The benefit of assessing [time] is it makes you think about motivation... That is useful, and thinking about the future, what's your motivations for spending time on things and how is that going to look in relation to everything else.
>
> - Gary

Gary found the time lens to be a motivating feature of the network of enterprises, particularly for future planning. Gary identified benefits, including how the tool could be used to strategise better for the future. Gary found this introspective process to be not merely about tracking hours or minutes but as an exercise in understanding the deeper 'why' behind engagement in enterprises, which can help to confront the underlying reasons for commitments, be it passion, obligation, or external rewards. For Gary, this lens becomes a valuable exercise in self-awareness that prompted a critical evaluation of whether his current engagement in enterprises is sustainable and beneficial in the long run. Gray found that a limitation of assessing significance was that visually this might look a bit block-y and therefore difficult to make the difference between time spent on different enterprises clear.

Remuneration

The remuneration lens was introduced as assessing enterprise significance in terms of how much money you make from each. The extract below outlines Heather's experiences with this lens. This was the least selected lens by FE teachers and trainers who have used the tool; it was suggested that, if you were interested in, or motivated by money, you probably would not be working in FE.

> There'll always be things that you have to do for money, so there'll always be things under remuneration for survival… that bring you limited joy.
> - Heather

Heather took a pragmatic approach and acknowledged the necessity of engaging in some enterprises for financial survival. While these enterprises might bring limited joy, Heather noted they may still hold inherent significance. Significance may relate to long-term benefits, including growth opportunities and goal achievement, both of which develop a professional identity over time. Overall, it is acknowledged that even the most mundane tasks can be integral to overall success and professional identity.

Passion

The passion lens was introduced as assessing enterprise significance in terms of how passionate you are about each. The extract below outlines Toby's experiences with this lens.

> Being involved in an activity… wanting to invest in that activity [and] wanting to invest yourself into that activity. I think passion is what I'm looking for in my… career and my teaching identity.
> - Toby

Toby used the passion lens, as for him passion fuels his motivation and commitment to teach. Toby seeks to integrate passion into his career, and the use of this lens enables him to find and maintain this. Toby's perspective highlights the importance of not just participating in an enterprise but investing fully into it. His enterprises provide him with a sense of purpose and fulfilment that results in his professional identity.

Personal

The personal lens was introduced as assessing enterprise significance in terms of the personal impact each enterprise has on you. The extract below outlines Beth's experiences with this lens.

> I could imagine having it at home... and looking at it through a personal [lens]... like the kind of practicalities... we'd be thinking about... how much time I'd have to invest and the impact on the family. It's not that we wouldn't also be talking about what I'm passionate about... but there are other... priorities that in that context.
>
> - Beth

Beth used the personal lens to consider the impact of enterprises on home life. For Beth, several considerations come into play, including time and passion, financial, emotional, and the physical resources required for each enterprise. Beth found that in this context there was a need for enterprises to be aligned with personal values. Beth considers the use of this lens with her partner as she explored how enterprises might influence family dynamics, with practical considerations on how enterprises would affect their daily routine and overall life balance. For Beth, benefits of this lens included that it made her consider her values and how her enterprises match up with these. FE teachers and trainers who engaged with this lens felt it could have a positive impact on teacher retention, helping individuals to reassess and evaluate their professional identities.

Professional

The professional lens was introduced as assessing enterprise significance in terms of the impact each has on your professional identity. The extract below outlines Beth's experiences with this lens.

> It would be really helpful for where I am now as I feel in limbo in terms of what I want to do... I think it would really help me; it would force me to try and think with some clarity and think critically and analytically about the pros and cons of choices.
>
> - Beth

Beth outlined that this lens was useful for systematically assessing the pros and cons of engagement in enterprises in terms of professional identity. Beth highlighted several key benefits of the professional lens, including its ability to facilitate greater clarity, sense of direction, and purpose. This lens allowed Beth to adopt a critical and analytical mindset, with the lens making her consider the broader impact of her involvement in enterprises. FE teachers and trainers who have used this lens found it easy to engage with, stating that as teachers or trainers they often reflect in this way. Beth felt that a difficulty of this lens might come in being indecisive and suggested that the tool could be useful within mentoring or coaching conversations.

FUTURE PLANNING

The final stage of the network of enterprise introduced to FE teachers and trainers was future planning. This stage includes looking one-to-five years ahead; setting the level of significance you hope each enterprise will hold, using the same lens you used when constructing the network of enterprises; planning your CPD activity with the network of enterprises; and revisiting and judging your success. The extract below outlines Kerry, Gary, and Heather's experiences with future planning.

> If I can see where I want to be, I never assume I'm going to get there, but I can assume I'll do my damned best to get there.
>
> - Kerry

Kerry highlighted the crucial role of future planning on her professional identity and the importance of having a clear vision for where she wants to be. For Kerry the network of enterprises allowed her to foster a forward-looking mindset, which helped her to articulate and map out her future aspirations. By making visual her desired outcomes, Kerry was able to create a tangible representation, which served as both a motivational anchor and a strategic guide. FE teachers and trainers who have used the tool identified benefits of this stage including the embedded accountability, the ability to work with goals in mind, the ability to develop useful and helpful habits, the ability to break things down into little steps, and the ability to be realistic about the future.

> I can see how this might be a really useful tool [for PhD students] because they might currently be in a teaching role but want to move into a research role and then you can see how that shift might happen over the three, four, five years of doctoral study.
>
> - Gary

Gary recognised the potential of the network of enterprises for future planning, particularly for PhD students navigating their academic and career trajectories. Gary highlighted that in this transitional period, the tool can be used to visualise and map career shifts which see some enterprises shrink and others grow, which might aid in planning for the future steps necessary to achieve a desired professional identity. The network of enterprises can help learners make informed decisions about their time and resource allocation, as well as help them anticipate potential challenges, reducing the uncertainty often associated with future planning. However, FE teachers and trainers who have used the tool identified a limitation, that life is unpredictable and sometimes you cannot plan for everything or achieve all you have set out to. Additionally, it was noted that engagement in the tool requires time and effort. While considered time-consuming, the tool was also considered to be easy to engage with, particularly when looking around three years ahead, as it provided them with structure and allowed them to think about different enterprises, helping them to build up a picture of their professional identity.

> I really love that visual... I really read it and understand it... Sometimes we focus on the small entities rather than the big picture.
>
> - Heather

The tool enhanced Heathers understanding and engagement of her career path. Heather expressed a strong appreciation for the visual aspect of the network of enterprises for future planning and she found that it aided her in comprehending the broader picture of her professional identity and to see how individual enterprises fit within it. Some FE teachers and trainers who used the tool suggested that future planning might led to frustration if they are not where they want to be professionally and/or do not have access to the resources and/or opportunities they need to change this and reach their preferred professional identity.

CONCLUSION

Overall, the network of enterprises was well-received, easily engaged with, and made FE teachers and trainers consider their professional identities. FE teacher and trainer engagement in the network of enterprises has shown it to be beneficial for those across the FE sector, in different stages and phases of their careers as professional identity is an ongoing concern. The tool has shown itself to aid not only in self-reflection but also in strategic planning, helping the FE teachers and trainers who engage with it identify their core strengths and areas of sustained interest while acknowledging the diverse enterprises that enrich their professional identity. The extract below outlines Elizabeths concluding thoughts.

> I think it'll be very interesting to see a visual representation... I imagine [it will be] a bit messy, really, but there'll be a straight line running through it, which will be teaching, and it will be my subject... but there'll be quite a lot of off shoots.
>
> - Elizabeth

Elizabeth expressed a keen interest in seeing a visual representation of her professional identity and felt that this provided a valuable insight into her career path. For Elizebeth the tool has the ability to reveal clear central themes of her

FROM USE TO INSIGHT

professional identity, her commitment to teaching, and her subject area, while also embracing the messiness of a lived life. The tool is also able to eloquently highlight the multifaceted nature of Elizabeth's professional identity and the breadth of enterprises she is engaged in. Elizibeth believes that the network of enterprises has the potential to clarify and organise her professional narrative, with the tool able to show her a path to continuity amidst the apparent complexity.

I will end this chapter with Kerry's completed networks of enterprises and final thoughts on using the tool by Kerry and Jason (Figure 4.1).

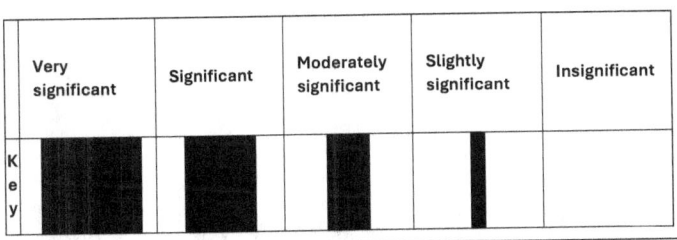

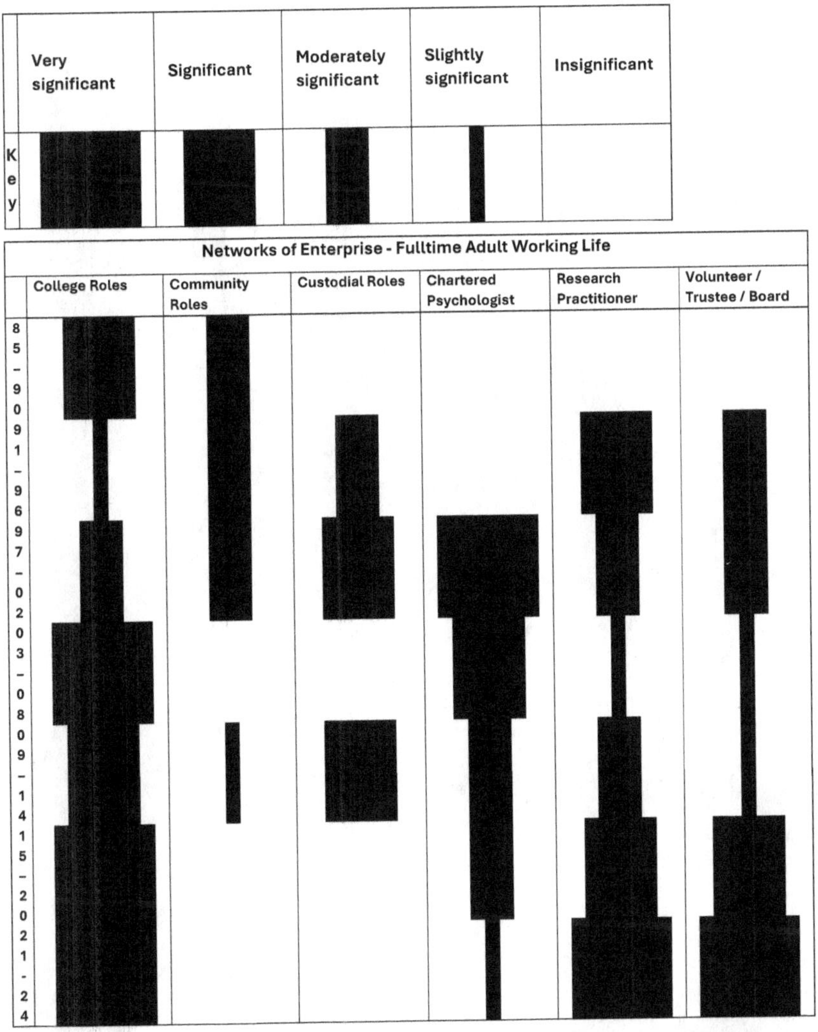

FIGURE 4.1 Kerry's network of enterprises.

77

> Sitting down to commit [to the network of enterprises] really makes you think... We need to sit down and think more... and focus the mind.
>
> - Jason

> When I settled on the five-year blocks, I found it really straightforward to use... the actual mechanics of it are great in the simplicities... It's absolutely brilliant in its simplicity because of the conversations you can have when you're creating it and then when you've got it, to interpret. The tool itself is very straightforward, [and] that invites human complexity to be applied to the tool... depending on how complex you want it to be.
>
> - Kerry

SECTION 1

Conclusion

Vignette: Who I am

I am an artist, I am a teacher, I am a researcher, I am a student.
Cairns, A. (2024) Who I am. Unpublished vignette.

Section 1 outlined the concept of multifaceted professional identities in the context of vocational and technical FE teachers and trainers. This section drew inspiration from the work of Wallace and Gruber (1989) and their tool, the network of enterprises. Section 1 showed the network of enterprises as a tool for tracking and charting identities over time and introduced its early use with creative people at work. Additionally, this section looked at Daichendt's (2011) use of the tool with artist-educator George Wallis, offering a case study from history as well as providing new case studies showing the network of enterprises updated use with technical and vocational FE teachers and trainers: Audrey Fairgrieve, Beth Curtis, Dr Gary Husband, Elizabeth Draper, Heather Booth-Martin, Jason Boucher, Kerry E Heathcote, and Toby Doncaster. This section ended with an opportunity to create your own network of enterprises to allow you to develop a better understanding of the complex mix of enterprises that make up your professional identity.

Section 1: 5 key take aways

- Multifaceted identities can be understood as a complex mix of diverse enterprises that come together to build a sense of self.
- Multifaceted identities can be and can feel complicated, but reflective practice can help you make sense of the situation.
- Within your FE teacher or trainer identity, you might hold multiple sub-identities that you must juggle.
- Networks of enterprises provide a simplified overview of engagement in different enterprises with a focus on goal achievement.
- Networks of enterprises are most useful when used as a person-centred tool for refection and future planning.

If you did not complete the *Try This!* activities as you read the chapter, I encourage you to go back and try them now. These activities have been designed to help you consider your professional identity, and engagement in them can form part of your reflective practice.

REFERENCES

Daichendt, G. J. (2011) 'The nineteenth-century artist-teacher: A case study of George Wallis and the creation of a new identity', *International Journal of Art and Design Education*, 30(1), pp. 71–80. doi: 10.1111/j.1476-8070.2011.01673.x.

Wallace, D. B., and Gruber, H. E. (1989) *Creative people at work: Twelve cognitive case studies*. New York: Oxford University Press.

SECTION 2

Likert Scales for Dual Identities introduction

Section 2: Likert Scales for Dual Identities introduction

> **Vignette: I can do both**
>
> Juggling two identities was at times exhausting and at times fulfilling. I quickly found a pattern of teaching and making art, artmaking, and teaching. I needed to prove to myself that I could teach and have an art practice. I can have an art practice and teach.
>
> Cairns, A. (2022) I can do both. Unpublished vignette.

This section outlines the concept of dual identities and dual professionalism in the context of vocational and technical FE teachers and trainers. This section draws inspiration from the work of James Daichendt (2009) on identity continuums and Alan Thornton (2013) and his concept of two identities coming together to form a dual identity. Likert Scales for Dual Identities are presented as a tool for capturing identity flux, originally used with artist-teachers (Cairns, 2023). Within this section, the Likert Scales for Dual Identities has been updated for use across vocational and technical disciplines.

This section is broken down into four chapters: Chapter 1 focuses on dual identities and how these are made up, by bringing two professional identities together (Graham and Rees, 2014). The chapter comments on how this experience might cause conflict between the two identities. Chapter 2 looks at what the Likert Scales for Dual Identities is and why it is important to those with dual identities. In this chapter, the tool is outlined as one used to chart current and ideal identities as well as one that shows how dual identities ebb and flow over time. Chapter 3 outlines how to use a Likert Scale for Dual Identities effectively and comprises a step-by-step guide for using the tool. Steps outlined include naming your identities, picking a numerical scale, picking a colour scheme, placement on the Likert Scale for Dual Identities, usage and averages, reflection, and future planning. The chapter ends with the opportunity to follow these steps to create your own Likert Scale for Dual Identities. Chapter 4 shares reflections from FE teachers and trainers and their use of the Likert Scales for Dual Identities. Joyce I-Hui Chen, Ronnie Houselander-Cook, and Sue Chillingworth share their insights.

REFERENCES

Cairns, A. (2023) *Interrogating artist-teacher identity transformation in adult community learning.* Doctoral thesis, Norwich University of the Arts.

Daichendt, G. J. (2009) 'Redefining the artist-teacher', *Journal of Art Education,* 62(5), pp. 33–38. doi: 10.1080/00043125.2009.11519035.

Graham, M., and Rees, J. (2014) 'Pick-up sticks art teacher-interconnectedness and fragility: Pedagogy as an artistic encounter', *Teaching Artist Journal,* 12(1), pp.15–23. doi: 10.1080/15411796.2014.844625.

Thornton, A. (2013) *Artist, researcher, teacher: A study of professional identity in art and education.* Chicago: University of Chicago Press.

CHAPTER FIVE

Dual identities

VIGNETTE: HOT AND COLD

There are several differences between being an artist and being a teacher. Some of these make doing both difficult, others make doing both easier. The oddest difference is that of heat. The relationship between being cold and being an artist has grown with me. Studios are cold and the heating is left off to save money. Juxtapose this with my experience of teaching in community learning. The classroom is warm and welcoming. I am always too hot. This might seem like an insignificant observation, but it serves as a visceral reminder of how different the two roles can be to embody.

Cairns, A. (2024) Hot and cold. Unpublished vignette.

INTRODUCTION

This chapter introduces the concept of dual professional identities and what this term means for vocational and technical FE teachers and trainers in the UK. I begin by explaining the term before drawing on the work of Plowright and Barr (2012) to situate it within an educational context. Reference is also made to the work of researchers who write on the topic of teachers and multifaceted identities (Robson, 1998; Daley et al., 2017; Loo, 2022).

This chapter draws on three key areas outlining dual professional identities, widely and more specifically concerning FE teachers and trainers; the notion of dual identities existing on continuums; the conflict that can occur between two roles; and what motivates you to embody this professional identity.

> ### TRY THIS! REFLECTING ON YOUR DUAL PROFESSIONAL IDENTITY IN TEACHING OR TRAINING
>
> Take a moment to reflect on your professional identity as a vocational or technical FE teacher or trainer. Consider the various roles, values, and experiences that shape your identity inside and outside the classroom. Use Table 5.1 to help you organise your thoughts and to identify specific aspects of your dual identity that you find challenging to navigate.
>
> Once you have completed the table (Table 5.1), explore how engaging in reflective practice helps you better understand and embrace your dual professional identity as a vocational or technical FE teacher or trainer. You may wish to consider how refection helps you navigate the complexities of your dual professional identity and how it enhances your self-awareness and understanding of your professional identity.
>
> **TABLE 5.1** Dual identity table
>
> | | *Vocational/ technical* | *Both* | *FE teaching/ training* |
> |---|---|---|---|
> | **Roles** | | | |
> | **Values** | | | |
> | **Experiences** | | | |

PART 1: DUAL IDENTITIES

Within this book, dual identities are understood in terms of professional identity, and your dual role is comprised of two inseparable and mutual components that come together to form a single identity (Wenger, 2000). The notion of dual professionalism is widely accepted within the FE sector (Robson et al., 2004) and is considered a key concept (Smithers, 2018). Dual professionals in the sector hold identities related to both vocational or technical specialism and teaching or training (McGowan, 2021). The two identities, or professions, may hold similar weight, importance, and time constraints, or one might be judged as holding more weight, being more important, or taking up more time. Section 1 explored multifaceted identities, and while you might hold many sub-identities, those with dual identities often identify more strongly with two of these, as they have more meaning to us than other sub-identities (Wenger, 2000).

This chapter explores dual identities from an educational perspective; there are other similar terms to dual identity that you might come across in the educational sector, including dual professionalism (Robson, 1998) and morphed professional (McGowan, 2021). Within the learning and skills sector dual professionals are understood as those qualified in a subject specialism and trained and committed to pedagogy (Plowright and Barr, 2012). You may still be working part-time in your vocational or technical area (Tummons, 2014; Fejes and Köpsén, 2014; Cairns, 2023b) or maybe trained in a vocational or technical area that you are no longer actively engaged in (Smithers, 2018; McGowan, 2021). It is important to note that it is not sufficient to only be an industry expert, and dual professionals in this context must also hold expertise in teaching or training (Antera and Teräs, 2024), as a key factor of this role is in demonstrating your dedication to both vocational or technical area and FE teaching or training (Thornton, 2013; ETF, 2022).

It is important to note that with dual identities, the two professional identities you hold may not necessarily work together, as the concept of dual identity can be seen as a dichotomy, with the two identities presented as opposed to each other (McGowan, 2021). However, others may find that there is indeed a synergy between the two identities and interaction between them which allows for a combined identity greater than either identity alone.

As a vocational or technical FE teacher or trainer you might find it relatively easy to identify your dual identity, as this is likely to be your vocational or technical identity and your FE teacher or trainer identity. However, if you are not teaching a subject related to your vocational or technical area, you may find Section 1 more useful. It is likely that as someone with a dual identity you are actively engaged with the communities of practice (CoP) associated with each of these identities (Wenger, 2000). Throughout your FE teaching or training career, you may experience one of three alliances with your vocational or technical area, at times you will find this is stronger than, weaker than, or equal to that of your alliance to FE teacher or trainer identity (Fejes and Köpsén, 2014), this is due to your dual role existing in a state of flux.

It is important to name your dual professional identity, as this allows you to name your reality and take control of it (Bucura, 2022). In choosing to hold a dual professional identity you are deciding to not abandon one identity, in favour of the other (Thornton, 2013). Bucura (2022) suggests that we should avoid looking at our identities in terms of either/or and embrace our dual identities as one whole, for example, I am an artist-teacher, I do not have to be an artist *or* a teacher. In naming this, as I do with the hyphenated term, I take ownership of my dual professional identity. When naming yourself and your dual professional identity grammatical choices may become important to ensure that the name you chose is not misunderstood by others. You may choose to hyphenate the two roles, as I do, or you may not. However, consider that hyphenating terms has the benefits of linking the two identities together and acknowledging the duality of the role (Page, 2012). Alternatively, you may feel that in the context you are working in this is implicit and that the two roles are automatically linked, leaving the hyphen redundant (Thornton, 2013).

Due to this linking of identities, vocational and technical FE teachers and trainers may be considered as dual citizens (Graham and Rees, 2014), as individuals who might teach or train in the day and engage in their vocational or technical area in the evening or in any other spare time. It is likely individuals will continue to work within their vocational or technical area, at least at the start of their FE teaching or training career, on a part-time basis (Tummons, 2014). You may find it beneficial to remain active to allow your knowledge in your specialist area to continue to develop, which in turn helps develop your teaching or training practice.

Within an educational context, vocational and technical FE teachers and trainers who hold a dual professional identity can act as a bridge between vocational or technical area and education (Peri et al., 2024). This should be viewed as a benefit of the role for the FE sector (Robson, 1998); as with your dual professional identity, you bring new and up-to-date knowledge and understanding (ETF, 2022), and you can expose learners to aspects of your field based on your lived experiences (Fejes and Köpsén, 2014). You may find that your former vocational or technical area even influences the way in which you teach or train (McGowan, 2021), as your teacher or trainer identity emerges out of your vocational or technical identity (Thornton, 2013).

TRY THIS! NAME YOUR DUAL IDENTITY

Explore how you might name your dual professional identity. You may wish to consider how your linguistic choices show your identification with both practices (Thronton, 2012), including whether you identify as a teacher or trainer, educator, facilitator, practitioner, or something else. When naming your dual professional identity, question how this communicates a commitment to both roles and if this commitment is equally split or if your priorities, attitudes and approaches to each identity vary (Daichendt, 2010).

PART 2: DUAL IDENTITY CONTINUUMS

A continuum refers to a continuous range of elements that blend into each other, often without abrupt changes or distinct boundaries. Within this book, identity continuums are used metaphorically to describe any gradual or continuous progression such as the continuum between vocational or technical and FE teacher or trainer identities. Within an identity continuum, your vocational or technical identity is placed at one end and your FE teacher or trainer identity at the other. You may find that the first position, situated on the left-hand side of the continuum, is that of your vocational or technical identity and that the second position, on the right-hand side, is your FE teacher or trainer identity (Smithers, 2018). It is somewhere in the middle of these two poles that your dual professional identity forms (Roller, 2013).

You may find yourself at either end of your dual professional identity continuum or somewhere in the middle at any time. Often, vocational and technical FE teachers and trainers do not identify strongly with one profession over the other (Fejes and Köpsén, 2014). However, initially you may feel that your two identities are distinct from one another (McGowan, 2021), for example, when you first move from your vocational or technical area to FE teaching or training, you may find that you have a strong vocationalist or technicalist identity, as this is the professional location that you have spent the most time in (Briggs, 2007) and the subject that you hold specialist knowledge in (Robson, 1998). You may have found each course you engage in acts as a catalyst for changing your professional identity (Thornton, 2013); this is because engagement in education and training, or any form of learning, is one way in which we construct our identities (Wenger, 2000). Transition to a dual professional identity, upon moving into teaching or training, may not be immediate and you may find that once you begin teaching or training in FE you need to first identify as solely a teacher or trainer before you can identify as a dual professional.

Viewing dual professional identities as a continuum allows the vocational or technical FE teacher or trainer to identity as both (Fejes and Köpsén, 2014), removing the need to pick between the two. Often the activities of each practice can support the other, and your dual professional identity is likely to blend more as you spend more time in a FE teacher or trainer professional location (Briggs, 2007). Once you have arrived at a dual professional identity, somewhere in the middle of your dual identity continuum, you will find that both are always involved in what you do, to different degrees (Wenger, 2000). Vocational and technical FE teachers and trainers are likely to retain a strong relationship with their vocational or technical area and the accompanying professional identity; this in turn will impact their emerging FE teacher or trainer identity (Robson et al., 2004).

As a dual professional you will be required to have knowledge of both and to bring these bodies of knowledge together (Plowright and Barr, 2012). There is a need for vocational and technical FE teachers and trainers to be both experts in subject matter and in pedagogy (Briggs, 2007), and existing on a continuum allows for this. Often vocational and technical FE teachers and trainers find working in FE to be an effective way to keep in touch with their vocational or technical area (Fejes and Köpsén, 2014). Your dual professional identity also benefits your learners, allowing you to become a useful teaching or training resource in the classroom (Peri et al., 2024). To further this connection, you may find it useful to explore your vocational or technical identity in relationship to your teacher or trainer identity and to consider the relationship between the two (Bucura, 2022).

It should be noted that dual professional identities are flexible, and you may find that your identity moves across the continuum depending on the context, or professional location, that you find yourself, with differing professional locations requiring you to be more of a vocationalist or technicalist or more of an FE teacher or trainer (Menter, 2023), due to identity being formed socially (Wenger, 2000). However, as a dual professional you must consider your placement on your identity continuum, as a too strong alliance with your first career may prevent you from identifying as an FE teacher or trainer (Orr and Simmons, 2010), as you develop your professional identity you must resist being pulled in the direction of either end of your continuum (Shreeve, 2009). You may find that your experience of existing on a continuum is not smooth, and if you find that your two identities are not compatible considerations may be needed as you bring the two together (Robson, 1998). FE teachers and trainers often find that their teacher or trainer identity overshadows their vocational or technical identity (Daichendt, 2010), and it can be useful to consider how your two identities overlap and what their relation to one another is to overcome this (McGowan, 2021). If you find yourself in the middle of your identity continuum you may find that your two identities have morphed into one, which may feel less conflicting (2021).

> **TRY THIS! EXPLORING YOUR DUALITY**
>
> Reflect on when you became a dual vocational or technical FE teacher or trainer by answering the questions provided below. It might be useful to consider if embracing your dual professional identity liberates or burdens you (Thornton, 2013). It is encouraged that you engage in reflective practice (Roller, 2013) as this can help you to come to terms with your dual professional identity. The questions below will go some way to facilitating this.

- **Background Questions:**
  - Can you recall a specific instance or event where you felt like a dual professional?
  - How did you feel during that moment?
- **Contextual Questions:**
  - Did this take place in your vocational/technical or teaching/training professional location or somewhere else?
  - Were there any particular groups of people involved (students, colleagues)?
- **Professional Development Questions:**
  - How did this moment contribute to your growth as a vocational/technical FE teacher or trainer?
  - Did you receive any feedback or recognition during this moment?
- **Impact Questions:**
  - How did this moment impact you?
  - Did it reinforce your passion for teaching/training your vocational/technical area in the FE sector?
- **Personal Reflection Questions:**
  - How did this moment align your two professional identities?
  - How has this moment shaped your identity as a vocational or technical FE teacher or trainer?
- **Future Implications Questions:**
  - How do you think this moment will influence your future teaching or training practices?
  - How will you continue to embrace your dual professional identity?

PART 3: IDENTITY CONFLICT

While this book celebrates dual identities the concept itself is not innately a positive one, and in some circumstances, it may even be considered as negative. This brings us to the concept of identity conflict or similar terms such as identity confusion (Erikson, 1994) and identity dissonance (Steadman, 2023) and comes from trying to balance two professional identities (Steadman, 2023). Steadman (2023) suggests that conflict is inherent to the teacher or trainer identity, which she outlines as an impossible profession due to the differences between FE teaching and training and vocational and technical experiences. These differences cause strain due to the contradictions between the two professional identities (Plowright and Barr, 2012). These have been described as binary tensions (Hofess, 2015) and may relate to the tensions between practical skills and pedagogical approaches, traditional teaching or training methods and innovative approaches from industry, and evolving technologies, due to these factors tensions are likely to be ongoing (Robson et al., 2004).

Conflict arises due to your dual professional identities comprising of competing roles, values, and loyalties (Robson et al., 2004; McGowan, 2021, Steadman, 2023). Additionally, conflict may arise due to the differing status of each role, their salaries (Antera and Teräs, 2024), the priority you give to each, and the amount of time spent on each (Bremmer et al., 2020). The conflict between vocational or technical roles and teaching or training appears to be deep-rooted with the classic rhetoric of 'those who can, do; those who can't, teach' (Shaw, 1903) and the tradition of placing more value on vocational or technical skills than on teaching or training, creating a problematic hierarchical relationship between the two that can cause conflict for those in the dual role (Steadman, 2023). If you find that you hide your teacher or trainer identity from others, you are not alone, with some vocational and technical teachers and trainers feeling a sense of failing their first career (Hatfield et al., 2006) and a feeling of a loss of credibility in their first field by colleagues in that field (Fejes and Kopsen, 2014). This threat to identity can lead to a split between your two professional identities and a reduced sense of self (Shreeve, 2009).

Identity conflict is most likely to take place during your transition period in becoming an FE teacher or trainer (McGowan, 2021), as periods of change often cause us feelings of identity conflict as any change in our sense of selves can cause discomfort (Steadman, 2023). The speed in which this change happens is also a factor in how much identity conflict is caused and how overwhelming we find it (Wenger, 2000), with teacher training courses often taking place as intensive, short experiences (Thornton, 2013). Additionally, the transition to identifying as an FE teacher or trainer has been linked to feelings of abandonment of a first identity tied to a vocational or technical area (Bremmer et al., 2020). However, this transformation is often an individual choice, linked to your personal and professional development (Thornton, 2013). Regardless of transition being by choice, or any other factor, the move from one professional identity to another or a dual professional identity is unlikely to be straightforward (Robson et al., 2004), as it also sees you join new CoP which is another demanding transformation for you to undertake (Wenger, 2000). This is pertinent for those who leave their vocational or technical area to join the FE workforce. However, those who continue to do both may find that continuing engagement in a dual professional identity can also cause tensions (Plowright and Barr, 2012). Conflict often arises due to time constraints and how dual professionals split their time between the two (Thornton, 2013), and this is challenging as your vocational or technical identity is contending with your new pedagogised identity (Page, 2012). This may leave you with a feeling of disconnect from yourself (Bremmer et al., 2020); to overcome this, pick a strategy that best allows you to maintain a sense of equilibrium in your life (Roller, 2013).

Identity conflict can be overcome, but to do this you will need to develop ways to enact each identity successfully (Kong, 2018). Your engagement in reflective practice will be invaluable here (Steadman, 2023), and an understanding that some form of sacrifice or compromise will be required on your part is key (Thornton, 2013). You might find it easier to hold two distinct identities (Robson et al., 2004), or you might form a new singular identity that encompasses both (Smithers, 2018), in either instance, the notion of reshaping your professional identity is central (Steadman, 2023), and you will need to learn to flow in and through each professional identity in different contexts (Hofess, 2015). It will also be beneficial to ensure that you are operating in contexts that validate both of your identities simultaneously, as if your identities are not validated by those around you, you are likely to stop enacting them (Hatfield et al., 2006). Support for both roles can help here, such as subject-specific CPD activities or learning opportunities (Clews and Clews, 2010).

TRY THIS! OVERCOMING IDENTITY CONFLICT

Consider ways in which you might overcome identity conflict, if you are facing it now or if you might face it in the future. You may currently be or have previously questioned if it is possible to balance two professional identities, and if they are compatible (Robson, 1998). One way of overcoming identity conflict is to focus on the positive relationship between your vocational or technical area and FE teaching or training practices (Thornton, 2013).

For each of your identities create a list of ten words you associate with it (Table 5.2). Once each list is completed review both list of words and see how many are the same or similar and which are different. Spend some time reflecting on the words that appear to conflict with each other and consider how you might challenge this limiting assumption. By acknowledging these differences and challenging assumptions, you can appreciate the diverse perspectives that your vocational or technical area and FE teacher or trainer identities bring to various situations.

TABLE 5.2 Overcoming identity conflict table

Vocational/technical	FE teacher/trainer
1.	1.
2.	2.
3.	3.
4.	4.
5.	5.
6.	6.
7.	7.
8.	8.
9.	9.
10.	10.

Similarities:

Differences:

PART 4: MOTIVATIONS FOR DUAL IDENTITIES

Motivation is the driving force behind the things we choose to do and can be intrinsic, driven by internal consequences, or extrinsic, related to external rewards (Deci, 2012). This section looks at what motivates us to become FE teachers or trainers and what motivates us to continue in the role as well as what threatens our motivation to teach or train in FE. You may have been motivated to join FE by one factor but motivated to continue by another, as motivators are likely to change over a career (Brooks, 2016). Steadman (2023) believes that the motivations of teachers and trainers have long been overlooked. However, it might be assumed that many go into teaching or training for altruistic reasons that affect others positively, such as serving others in the community (Monereo, 2022) and helping students progress (Bucura, 2022), which are aligned with the want to improve the lives of others and make a difference in the world (Steadman, 2023).

We will first look at motivations for entering teaching or training. Motivations are likely to vary between individuals (Menter, 2023); however, it is suggested that those who enter FE are often strongly motivated by social justice issues (Daley et al., 2017). FE teachers and trainers are often service-orientated (Menter, 2023). Motivation may also come from a strong sense of vocational or technical identity and a desire to share your vocational or technical expertise (Brooks, 2016). For FE teachers and trainers intrinsic motivations are often fuelled by personal fulfilment and internal states that feel rewarding (Deci 2012), for example, you may be motivated to teach or train as you believe it will enhance your own practice (Thornton, 2013; Brooks, 2016). Other reasons may include being motivated by your own FE teachers or trainers (Daichendt, 2010) or a desire to share your passion, enthusiasm, and knowledge for your vocational or technical area with others (Daley et al., 2017; Menter, 2023). However, some motivators are more extrinsic, such as moving into FE due to perceived job security (Loo, 2022) or a move into a new, possibly salaried career that is seen to be more viable than roles in your vocational or technical area (Bucura, 2022). An often-dominant way for understanding extrinsic motivation for entering FE teaching or training is related to remuneration – financial reward (Thornton, 2013), which can be understood as an external incentive motivator (Deci, 2012). However, the truth of this is worth considering, with the low pay of the FE sector (Augar Review, 2019).

Motivations to continue to teach have been attributed to feelings of job satisfaction (Thornton, 2013) and to feeling valued by colleagues in both their vocational or technical contexts and teacher or trainer contexts (Hatfield et al., 2006). While feelings of satisfaction related to intrinsic motivation, feeling valued is more extrinsic, as it relies on others and their actions towards us (Deci, 2012). You may also be motivated by the thought of further progressing your FE role through future training as well as your own personal and professional growth (Menter, 2023), and these are examples of intrinsic competence motivation, related to the enjoyment of learning (Deci, 2012). You may also find the learners that you work with are a motivating factor to stay in your role (Bucura, 2022; Cairns, 2023a). A prolonged interest in your vocational or technical area can also serve as motivation to continuing teaching or training on the subject in FE (Brooks, 2016) as well as opportunities to further explore new developments within the field (Bucura, 2022).

Throughout your FE teaching or training career, you may face threats to your motivation. These can stem from a lack of autonomy in your teaching role, which can negatively impact how motivated you are (Daley et al., 2017). Autonomy is deemed essential to individuals continuing to undertake an activity, lack of autonomy is linked to feelings of being unvalued or under-valued (Daley et al., 2017), and this is a very real threat to FE teachers and trainers, with those in the sector described as the most devalued public sector workers

(Westminster Hall, 2021). Your motivation may also be threatened by high workloads, a focus on meeting targets, working in a high stress environment, and emotional exhaustion (Menter, 2023).

> ### TRY THIS! YOUR MOTIVATIONS FOR DOING THE WORK
>
> Reflect on your motivations for becoming a dual professional (Steadman, 2023). Motivation can be a complicated area to unpack as it relies on you understanding exactly what it is that makes you do particular things (Kong, 2018). However, understanding your motivation can be extremely useful as this plays a big part in your identity, and what makes you the vocational or technical FE teacher or trainer that you are (Monereo, 2022). Understanding your motivations allows you to understand what activities you make the most meaning from (Menter, 2023), and the questions below will go some way to facilitating this meaning making.
>
> - **Background Questions:**
>   - Can you recall a specific instance or event that sparked your motivation to become an FE teacher or trainer?
>   - How did you feel during that moment, and what drove you towards pursuing a career in FE teaching or training?
> - **Contextual Questions:**
>   - Did this motivation originate from experiences within your vocational/technical or teaching/training professional environment, or did it stem from elsewhere?
>   - Were there any specific individuals or groups who influenced your decision to pursue a career in FE teaching or training?
> - **Professional Development Questions:**
>   - How did this initial motivation contribute to your development as an FE teacher/trainer in the vocational/technical field?
>   - Did you receive any guidance or support in nurturing this motivation?
> - **Impact Questions:**
>   - How has this initial motivation influenced your journey as an FE teacher or trainer?
>   - In what ways has this motivation shaped your identity and commitment as an FE teacher or trainer?
> - **Personal Reflection Questions:**
>   - Looking back, how does this initial motivation align with your current motivations as an FE teacher or trainer?
>   - How has this initial motivation evolved or been sustained throughout your career in FE teaching or training?

- **Future Implications Questions:**
  - How do you believe this initial motivation will continue to drive your future teaching or training practices?
  - How do you plan to maintain and reinforce this motivation as you progress in your career as an FE teacher or trainer?

CONCLUSION

To conclude dual professional identities can be understood as the bringing together of two professional identities to create a new one. It was shown how vocational and technical FE teachers and trainers are often operating as dual citizens (Graham and Rees, 2014), who exist on a continuum. We have seen how having a dual professional identity may be a conflicting place to find yourself and how reflecting on your motivations for becoming and continuing to be an FE teacher or trainer may help you sustain the practice.

This chapter has shown how your identity might change throughout your professional career depending on personal choices and engagement in different activities, including training and education (Wenger, 2000). This chapter has highlighted that you may be expected to maintain subject specialist knowledge and skills as well as those related to pedagogy (ETF, 2022). Balancing dual identities can be difficult but rewarding. In the next chapter, we explore what the Likert Scales for Dual Identities is and why they are important in relation to dual identities.

REFERENCES

Antera, S., and Teräs, M. (2024) 'Discovering and developing the vocational teacher identity', *Education + Training*. doi: 10.1108/ET-09-2023-0363.

Augar Review (2019) *Independent panel report to the review of post-18 education and funding May 2019*. Available at: https://assets.publishing.service.gov.uk/government/uploads/system/uploads/attachment_data/file/805127/Review_of_post_18_education_and_funding.pdf (Accessed 23 February 2024).

Bremmer, M., Heijnen, E., and Kersten, S. (2020) 'Teacher as conceptual artist', *The International Journal for Art and Design Education*, 40(1), pp. 82–98. doi: 10.1111/jade.12318.

Briggs, A. R. J. (2007) 'Exploring professional identities: Middle leadership in further education colleges', *School Leadership and Management*, 27(5), pp. 471–485. doi: 10.1080/13632430701606152.

Brooks, C. (2016) *Teacher subject identity in professional practice: Teaching with a professional compass*. New York: Routledge.

Bucura, E. (2022) *Music teacher identities: Places, people, and practices of the professional self.* Münster: Waxmann Verlag GmbH.

Cairns, A. (2023a) 'What motivates the artist-teacher in adult community learning?', *Journal of Research in Post Compulsory Education,* 28(2). pp. 260–275. doi: 10.1080/13596748.2023.2206709.

Cairns, A. (2023b) *Interrogating artist-teacher identity transformation in adult community learning.* Doctoral thesis, Norwich University of the Arts.

Clews, A., and Clews, D. (2010) 'And I also teach: The professional development of teaching creatives', *Journal of Arts & Communities,* 1(3), pp. 265–278. doi: 10.1386/jaac.1.3.265_1.

Daichendt, G. J. (2010) *Artist-teacher: A philosophy for creating and teaching.* Bristol: Intellect.

Daley, M., Orr, K., and Petrie, J. (2017) *The Principal: Power and Professionalism in FE.* London: Trentham Books.

Deci, E. L. (2012) *Intrinsic motivation.* New York: Springer US.

Education and Training Foundation (ETF) (2022) *Professional standards for teachers and trainers in the further education and training sector.* Available at: https://www.et-foundation.co.uk/professional-standards/ (Accessed 27 April 2024).

Erikson, E. (1994) *Identity and the life cycle.* New York: W. W. Norton & Company.

Fejes, A., and Köpsén, S. (2014) 'Vocational teachers' identity formation through boundary crossing', *Journal of Education and Work,* 27(3), pp. 265–283. doi: 10.1080/13639080.2012.742181.

Graham, M., and Rees, J. (2014) 'Pick-up sticks art teacher-interconnectedness and fragility: Pedagogy as an artistic encounter', *Teaching Artist Journal,* 12(1), pp. 15–23. doi: 10.1080/15411796.2014.844625.

Hatfield, C., Montana, V., and Deffenbaugh, C. (2006) 'Artist/art educator: Making sense of identity issues', *Art Education,* 59(3), pp. 42–47. doi: 10.1080/00043125.2006.11651594.

Hofsess, B. A. (2015) 'The Map of True Places: Moving Onward in Artist-Teacher Preparation', *Visual Arts Research,* 41(1), p. 1. doi: 10.5406/visuartsrese.41.1.0001.

Kong, M. (2018) *The hopes and experiences of bilingual teachers of English: Investments, expectations and identity.* Abingdon: Taylor & Francis.

Loo, S. (2022) *Teacher educators in vocational and further education.* Cham. Switzerland: Springer International Publishing.

McGowan, A. (2021) *The professional identity of the further education teacher in the UK: A case study.* Ed.D thesis, Kingston University.

Menter, I. (2023) *The Palgrave handbook of teacher education research.* Cham: Springer International Publishing.

Monereo, C. (2022) *The identity of education professionals: Positioning, training, and innovation.* Charlotte: Information Age Publishing, Incorporated.

Orr, K., and Simmons, R. (2010) 'Dual identities: The in-service teacher trainee experience in the English further education sector', *Journal of Vocational Education & Training,* 62(1), pp. 75–88. doi: 10.1080/13636820903452650.

Page, T. (2012) 'A shared place of discovery and creativity: Practices of contemporary art and design pedagogy,' *International Journal for Art and Design Education,* 31(1), pp. 67–77. doi: 10.1111/j.1476-8070.2012.01732.x.

Peri, E., Jõgi, L., and Remmik, M. (2024) 'Who am I: Teacher or practitioner? Teacher-practitioners' experience of identity in higher education. A phenomenological view,' *Future on Educational Research,* 2(1), pp. 65–80. doi: https://doi.org/10.1002/fer3.20.

Plowright, D., and Barr, G. (2012) 'An integrated professionalism in further education: A time for phronesis?', *Journal of Further and Higher Education,* 36(1), pp. 1–16. dio: 10.1080/0309877X.2011.590584.

Robson, J. (1998) 'A profession in crisis: Status, culture and identity in the further education college', *Journal of Vocational Education and Training,* 50(4), pp. 585–607.

Robson, J., Bailey, B., and Larkin, S. (2004) 'Adding value: Investigating the discourse of professionalism adopted by vocational teachers in further education colleges', *Journal of Education and Work,* 17(2), pp. 183–195. doi: 10.1080/13639080410001677392.

Roller, N. G. (2013) *Understanding how the role of an artist-teacher may impact student learning and teaching practice.* Boston: Boston University Department of Art Education.

Shaw, G. B. (1903) *Man and superman.* New York: Brentano.

Shreeve, A. (2009) '"I'd rather be seen as a practitioner, come in to teach my subject": Identity work in part-time art and design tutors', *International Journal of Art & Design Education,* 28(2), pp. 151–159. doi: 10.1111/j.1476-8070.2009.01602.x.

Smithers, M. R. (2018) *Towards an understanding of the construction of the professional identity of vocational further education college teachers.* Doctoral thesis (Ed.D), London (University College London).

Steadman, S. (2023) *Identity: Keywords in teacher education.* London: Bloomsbury Academic.

Thornton, A. (2012) 'What is it to be an artist teacher in England today?', *World Journal of Education,* 2(6), pp. 39–44. doi: 10.5430/wje.v2n6p39.

Thornton, A. (2013) *Artist, researcher, teacher: A study of professional identity in art and education.* Chicago: University of Chicago Press.

Tummons, J. (2014) 'Professional standards in teacher education: Tracing discourses of professionalism through the analysis of textbooks', *Research in Post-Compulsory Education,* 19(4), pp. 417–432. doi: 10.1080/13596748.2014.955634.

Wenger, E. (2000) *Communities of practice: Learning meaning and identity.* Cambridge: University of Cambridge Press.

Westminster Hall (2021) *Westminster Hall debate: Third report of the education committee, A plan for an adult skills and lifelong learning revolution,* HC 278. 15 April 2021, 1,30pm. Available at: https://parliamentlive.tv/event/index/f3d210ee-0aab-4050-9fe5-e8b09e5f4ed2 (Accessed 15 April 2024).

CHAPTER SIX

What is the Likert Scale for Dual Identities and why is it important?

> **VIGNETTE: JUMP IN**
>
> Upon entering the PGCE I was already an artist, to some extent I always had been, and since completing my BA in fine art I also have a piece of paper to prove it. However, I was not a teacher and there was much to learn. Most of it quickly. This was knowledge that I needed to learn away from my artist self. I could not jump in, day one, and be an artist-teacher. I was confident as an artist but had no idea what I was doing as a teacher.
>
> Cairns, A. (2023) Jump in. Unpublished vignette.

INTRODUCTION

In this chapter, the Likert Scale for Dual Identities will be introduced and its importance to vocational and technical FE teachers and trainers will be explored. By the end of this chapter, you will be thoroughly informed about the tool and be in a better position to engage in its use.

This chapter first outlines the tool, before sharing its early use and history drawing on my work with artist-teachers working in adult community learning (ACL) (Cairns, 2023b). This chapter explores case studies of use from the published literature, which explores my use of the tool with research participants (2023a, 2023b). This chapter ends by outlining the limitations of the tool, before suggesting how an updated version of the Likert Scale for Dual Identities goes some way to overcome them.

PART 1: LIKERT SCALES FOR DUAL IDENTITIES

Part 1 explores the main themes of Likert Scales for Dual Identities. This work draws on my early research and exploration of dual identities with artist-teachers in ACL (Cairns, 2023b). Part 1 includes the original use of and purpose of the Likert Scale for Dual Identities, the importance of flux to the tool, how the significance of each identity changes between different contexts, and the role that continuums play, with reference to Daichendt (2009). The main purpose of the Likert Scale for Dual Identities is to provide a visual overview of an individual's dual professional identity and where they sit within the duality. As a tool, the Likert Scale for Dual Identities draws on the continuum-like nature of vocational and technical FE teachers and trainers, allowing the identity flux experienced by these individuals to be documented (Cairns, 2023b). The Likert Scale for Dual Identities comes with the assumption that you hold two distinct professional identities, that of FE teacher or trainer, and that of your vocational or technical area, and that you have access to the two differing contexts that these professional identities sit within.

Use and purpose

I first used the Likert Scales for Dual Identities, then named the Artist-Teacher Likert Scales, with artist-teachers working in ACL in the UK, as a post-graduate research student (Cairns, 2023a, 2023b). Within my study the tool was used to allow artist-teacher participants to plot their current and ideal identities. Additionally, the Artist-Teacher Likert Scale was used with managers of artist-teachers. Managers were asked to place an *ideal artist-teacher* on the scale between the points of teacher and artist. The tool was used within a social science study which aimed to understand and represent *the identity transformation of artist-teachers in ACL* (Cairns, 2023b). While my initial use of the tool was with a specific subgroup of vocational and technical FE teachers and trainers, this work led me to see how the tool might, with adaptations such as a change in the name, be useful to others in similar positions and contexts.

The intended use of the Artist-Teacher Likert Scale (Figure 6.1) was to explore how artist-teachers and their managers understood their dual identities. The tool was initially used as an interview tool to collect continuous data for analysis. The visual nature of the tool was intentional and intended to be engaging. Artist-teacher participants were asked to place themselves on a scale that went from teacher to artist conceptually and from one to ten numerically. The Artist-Teacher Likert Scale additionally incorporated a colour scheme, based on theorist Alan Thornton's (2013) artist-teacher model and colour-coding scheme in which he understands teachers as blue, artists as red, and artist-teachers as purple.

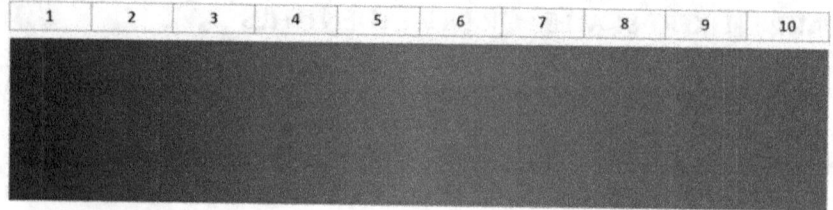

FIGURE 6.1 Reproduction of the Artist-Teacher Likert Scale in black and white (Cairns, 2023b).

The real-world applicability of the Artist-Teacher Likert Scale soon became clear (Nadler, 1980), as participants could easily place themselves on the tool to reflect their current and ideal identities. With this discovery, the tool went from being an interview aid to a person-centred tool for self-reflection. The Likert Scale for Dual Identities is suitable for not only artist-teachers but any professional who engages in two identities such as other vocational and technical FE teachers and trainers. The Likert Scale for Dual Identities can help those of us with dual identities to visualise our professional selves (Cairns, 2023a), by attaching current identities to specific anchors along a colourful continuum. Dual professionals are outlined as those with two professional locations in which they operate (Briggs, 2007). FE teachers and trainers are dual professionals as they operate in FE contexts and vocational or technical contexts. The tool has an emphasis on visual documentation of flux and engagement in self-reflection.

The design of the Likert Scale for Dual Identities allows for identity to be captured and for this to become documentation of how our identities ebb and flow over time (Steadman, 2023). As we move though our days, weeks, months, and years, our identities shift and documentation of professional identity grows over time; the Likert Scale for Dual Identities starts to show a clear understanding of our distinct professional identities (McAdams, 1993). The Likert Scales for Dual Identities visually shows when these shifts, up or down the continuum, occur, and self-reflection allows us to know why, often this is related to a shift in context or professional location (Briggs, 2007). This is true for the work of vocational and technical FE teachers and trainers who often have a vocational or technical location and a teaching or training location. Likert Scales for Dual Identities help to document how moving between contexts changes our identity, drawing on Pierre Bourdieu's (1990) ideas around structures, habitus, and practices and how the relationship between these three pillars is interactive and responsive, with structures shaping habitus and habitus shaping practice.

Documenting flux

Likert Scales for Dual Identities works on the belief that professional identities change frequently (Cairns, 2023b), and as a tool it has a focus on documenting this flux. By documenting your ideal and current identities you are better able to understand your professional identity. For vocational and technical FE teachers and trainers this might mean the ability to work towards their ideal professional identity through self-reflection and action.

Steadman (2023) outlines that teacher and trainer identity is always in flux as we navigate changes in our professional landscape. Dual professional identity flux takes place on a continuum (Daichendt, 2010) and is continuously shifting (Fejes and Köpsén, 2014). Flux is important, and those with dual professional identities, such as vocational and technical FE teachers and trainers, may find that at times, they need to embody one identity more than the other, depending on the professional context they find themselves in (Briggs, 2007). In this act of flux, we move between two fields (Daichendt, 2010), as we move from one profession to another or somewhere in between (Fejes and Köpsén, 2014). This movement allows you to engage in both identities to varying degrees depending on circumstances, often a necessity in contemporary society, which often requires us to hold opposing positions simultaneously (McAdams, 1993). Keeping track of your professional identity and how it changes allows you to continue to engage in two differing professions, helping you to embrace your dual professional identity.

The two identities named in your Likert Scale for Dual Identities will be your two most dominant professional identities; however, you might have other professional identities that you do not identify with as strongly or are not as dominant in your professional lives. To further explore your sub-identities, revisit the network of enterprises in Section 1. It should be noted that your dual identity might change over time, one such change could be a move from being a vocationalist-teacher to a teacher-educator or a move between teaching one vocational subject to another. For example, a move from an artist-teacher identity to a designer-teacher identity as your career develops and you engage in training and diverse communities of practice (CoP) (Wenger, 2000). However, there may be an assumption that the teacher part of your identity will remain, as a relativity stable part of your professional identity (McAdams, 1993).

One of the main benefits of having a dual professional identity is that you can engage in boundary crossing (Wenger, 2000). FE teachers and trainers tend to cross the boundaries between their vocational or technical practice and teacher or trainer practice (Fejes and Köpsén, 2014). This allows you to remain active in both professional identities and prevents you from having to engage in the *either/or* rhetoric (Thornton, 2013). Developments in each area can benefit the other as interactions between different practices result in learning (Fejes and Köpsén, 2014). As you engage with the Likert Scale for Dual Identities, your documented placements become an individualised picture of your changing professional identity that tells the story of your lived experiences (McAdams, 1993). The tool allows you to see if you are making progress towards your ideal identity, if your ideal identity changes, and how you are reacting to identity flux.

PART 2: EARLY USE AND A CASE STUDY FROM THE PUBLISHED LITERATURE

In my work (Cairns, 2023a, 2023b) I provide examples of my original tool, the Artist-Teacher Likert Scale, in use with 17 artist-teachers in ACL. Each case outlines the individual artist-teacher's current and ideal artist-teacher identity from their insider perspective. The tool was additionally used with seven managers of artist-teachers who used the tool to plot their *ideal artist-teacher*. Part 2 focuses on my work with artist-teachers, rather than their managers, as this book is aimed at those wishing to engage in self-reflection. There have been no other published uses of the tool outside of my study; however, there is earlier work published around dual identities existing on a continuum (Parker, 2009; Daichendt, 2009). Parker (2009) suggests vocational and technical teachers and trainers can place themselves on a continuum between their vocational or technical identity and teacher or trainer identity, placing himself as identifying more strongly as a teacher than as an artist. Additionally, Daichendt's (2009) work states that a dual professional's dual identity is formed in the middle of a continuum, between the two poles of vocationalist or technicalist and teacher or trainer, a concept that my work continues.

Background

In my use of the Artist-Teacher Likert Scale (Cairns, 2023a, 2023b) I held little prior knowledge of the artist-teacher participants I used it with, as the tool was intended to be used by the participants, I did not require a strong narrative insight into their lives at this point. The only prerequisite of use of the tool was knowing that they held the dual identity of artist-teacher and that they specifically taught within ACL. I used the Artist-Teacher Likert Scale to help chart participants' current and ideal identities before engaging in life story interviews with them to gain a narrative insight into why they placed themselves as they had (McAdams, 1993).

The tool was first introduced to participants in a pre-interview email, where they were informed that during the interview I would ask them to place themselves on the Artist-Teacher Likert Scale, within the email, the workings of the tool were explained, and an image of the tool was also included (Figure 6.1). At the beginning of the interview, I reintroduced the tool, sharing an image of it on screen and asking participants to place themselves on the scale between the two poles of teacher and artist. Once participants placed their current and ideal identities, they were asked to share why they placed themselves in this way. Later in my study artist-teacher participants were asked to comment on the real-life applicability of the tool (Nadler, 1980). Participants responded that the

Artist-Teacher Likert Scale was highly applicable to real life (Cairns, 2023b) and were drawn to four main aspects of the tool: its continuum nature, its ability to capture flux over different periods of time, it is a quick tool to engage with, and at its heart it is a visual tool. The colour scheme was particularly favoured, with the rationale that as artists they appreciated the use of colour (2023b).

Use

As I outline the use of the tool I will share results from the 17 artist-teachers who engaged in the tool, including their current and ideal artist-teacher identities, before sharing a more in-depth case study from an artist-teacher in ACL: Artist-Teacher V.

Statistics

Seventeen artist-teachers were invited to place themselves on the Artist-Teacher Likert Scale and were all successful in the task. Their responses were varied and highlight the legitimacy of holding an artist-teacher identity anywhere on the continuum. Some, like Parker (2009), identified more strongly as teachers, others as artists, and some more centrally. Some artist-teachers (n = 10) longed for change in their position, while others (n = 7) had already met their ideal dual professional identity (Figure 6.2).

	A	B	C	E	F	G	H	I	K	L	O	P	V	W	X	Y	Z
Current	5	5	8	9	8	5	3	4	6	7	6	4	3	8	6	3	7
Ideal	7	6	8	10	10	5	7	7	9	7	8	4	3	8	8	3	7

FIGURE 6.2 Artist-teachers' current and ideal identities.

While current identities were quite diverse, there was a trend for ideal identities being placed closer to the *artist* end of the continuum. However, the tool is intended to be useful for the individual, so comparisons between placements are not necessary here. Instead, I will outline how individual artist-teachers made use of the tool:

- Artist-Teacher W commented on how the Artist-Teacher Likert Scale made her consider where she is and where she would like to be, before concluding that she is where she would like to be.
- Artist-Teacher O considered the activities she was engaged in and how these would help her achieve her ideal identity. She felt that completing her practice-based PhD in fine art would help her move from a 6 to an 8 on the scale.
- Artist-Teacher A worried that by placing herself as a 5 she could be seen as not making a decision about her identity. However, how she splits her time across both professional identities reflects this mid-point.
- Artist-Teacher L was able to use the scale to communicate how her identity had fluctuated throughout her career. She shared that while she is currently placed at 7, she would have previously placed herself at 3 and has had times when she would have liked to be placed at 10.

CASE STUDY

Artist-Teacher V is a female-identifying 30–34-year-old based in East of England (Cairns, 2023b). Artist-Teacher V has been working in her role in ACL for one year, before joining the ACL workforce she worked in other community settings. Artist-Teacher V shares that she spends 95 per cent of her working time teaching and the other 5 per cent on her own art.

In her use of the tool, Artist-teacher V placed her current and ideal identities easily. She placed both her current and ideal identities as a three on the Artist-Teacher Likert Scale, more teacher. In her interview, Artist-Teacher V expressed that she wants others, including her learners and manager, to view her as a teacher, rather than as an artist. However, her use of the tool became more interesting when she engaged in self-reflection and added a personal narrative. Artist-Teacher V used the tool to look backward, and she stated that the Artist-Teacher Likert Scale allowed her to plot her journey and recognise that earlier in her career she would have identified more strongly as an artist. With use of the tool, Artist-Teacher V reflected on why this was, concluding that her teaching roles and responsibilities took over in terms of how she was spending her time. To illustrate this, she shared that she now spends her evenings completing paperwork related to her teaching role, rather than painting. The use of the Artist-Teacher Likert Scale facilitated this thinking as she was able to better visualise the movement between the two poles. Artist-Teacher V liked the visual aspect of the tool, and how movement was possible between teacher and artist, as she believes that her identity shifts depending on the time of the year.

Dual identity

Despite their differences, the results from the 17 artist-teachers and the case of Artist-Teacher V highlight how the Artist-Teacher Likert Scale allowed participants to track and chart their dual professional identities. The results show that the dual identity of the artist-teacher sits on a continuum between the two points of teacher and artist (Daichendt, 2009). The case of Artist-Teacher V highlights that dual identities are in flux depending on the different activities they engage in and even different times of the year or day (Thornton, 2013). The Artist-Teacher Likert Scale acknowledges identity flux and allows the user to place themselves differently each time they use it; this helps the individual to eloquently, and quickly, express their lived experiences of flux.

Flux becomes important for artist-teachers, and other vocational or technical teachers or trainers, with the ability to balance different activities central to teaching in FE. Those in a dual role, such as artist-teachers, are often expected to continue to engage in their practice outside of teaching (Daichendt, 2010). As with Artist-Teacher V, those with dual identities often find that they are juggling the roles and responsibilities of their vocational or technical area, with those of the teacher or trainer, more often than not it is the administrative work around teaching and training that those in the sector report to taking up their time, rather than teaching itself (Bishop, 2011).

The lived experiences of these 17 artist-teachers show that they do not have to choose between being an artist or a teacher (Thornton 2013). The Artist-Teacher Likert Scale allows those who engage with it to consider factors that may affect their dual professional identity and how this impacts how they see themselves. Dual identities are often shifting and can be complex to communicate and understand; however, the tool gives artist-teachers a way of visualising this thinking process of moving between professional identities and landing somewhere in the middle (Fejes and Köpsén, 2014). The 17 artist-teachers highlight that the experience of being an artist-teacher can differ from one artist-teacher to another; as artist-teacher identity is not one size fits all (Parker, 2009), dual identity does not have to look the same and artist-teachers can place themselves at either end of the scale or in the middle. Artist-teachers experience identity flux and may feel more like an 'artist' in one place and more like a 'teacher' in another. Additionally, artist-teachers are free to want to change the balance of their dual professional identity. Individuals can use the Artist-Teacher Likert Scale to evaluate their dual identity and act if needed. In engaging with the tool, artist-teachers can consider the ways they might want to change their identity, why they currently identify in the way they do, and the consequences of moving along the scale, in either direction.

PART 3: LIMITATIONS AND UPDATES

The Likert Scale for Dual Identities is not without its limitations; Part 3 explores these along with ways to overcome them. The limitations shared are drawn from my findings from my early use of the tool, then named the Artist-Teacher Likert Scale, with artist-teachers working in ACL in the UK (Cairns, 2023a, 2023b). Part 3 covers key limitations, including the ten-point scale used in the Artist-Teacher Likert Scale, the static nature of the tool, Likert scales and their link to maths, and its simplistic nature. Updates to the Likert Scale for Dual Identities include a move toward odd-numbered scales, a tool that encourages continuous documentation, textual anchors, and the importance of engaging in self-refection.

10-point scale

One of the main limitations of the Artist-Teacher Likert Scale was its use of a ten-point scale. The limitations of a ten-point or any evenly numbered scale include the inability to place yourself in the middle, forcing the user to make a choice and lean more in one direction over the other. For example, while Artist-Teacher A stated they felt in the middle of the scale by selecting 5 on the Artist-Teacher Likert Scale in Part 2, numerically they were not, as a 5 on a ten-point scale leans towards more teacher than artist. As a result, even numbered scales make nuance harder, force the user's hand, and can be more easily misinterpreted. The Likert Scale for Dual Identities has been updated and moves toward odd numbered scales, and the benefit of this is that it allows for neutrality, with a clear midpoint. Odd numbered scales provide balanced options and more flexibility and reduce forced choice, making them more accurate than their even-point counterparts.

Static tool

Participants in my early studies felt that the Artist-Teacher Likert Scale did not effectively capture flux and that the tool should become more overtly interactive to help document the day-to-day flux of the role. The original tool was presented one Likert scale at a time, with no record of how it had been interacted with previously. While most participants in my early studies understood that the tool could be re-used and identity replotted, Artist-Teacher Z felt that the flux was not documented or visualised effectively (Cairns, 2023b). However, her use of the tool highlighted that it could effectively help you place flux, as the first time Artist-Teacher Z engaged with the Artist-Teacher Likert Scale she put herself at 7, more artist. In her accompanying self-refection, Artist-Teacher Z stated that she felt more like an artist than a teacher as she was only mid-way through her BA in Education and she felt that she could not identify as a teacher as she had limited experience in this field and was teaching minimal hours. The next time she engaged with the tool, a few months later, she put herself at 4, more teacher. In her self-reflection, she stated that she had almost finished her BA and was teaching more hours. Artist-Teacher Z's identity had transformed, and the tool was able to capture this but not documented it. To overcome the issue of documenting flux, the updated Likert Scale for Dual Identities differs and allows a visual record to be kept (Figure 6.3). The tool can now be expanded each time it is engaged with, to capture flux over time.

Position: Me						
Ideal			x			
Artist	1	2	3	4	5	Teacher
1 2 3						

FIGURE 6.3 An example of a Likert Scale for Dual Identities.

Maths

Some users of the Artist-Teacher Likert Scale reported that the link between the tool and maths was off-putting due to personal negative feelings towards the subject. Additionally, it was considered that connecting your identity to a number might be an abstract activity to engage in. The updated Likert Scale for Dual Identities has been developed to include textual anchors tied to each numerical point, and these anchors offer brief descriptors of the identity linked to each number. Working with anchors can feel more concrete and provide a way into the tool for those who would rather work with language, than numbers.

A simple tool

While the simplistic nature of the Artist-Teacher Likert Scale was lauded by some, others felt that this resulted in the tool not covering many areas of professional identity. The updated Likert Scale for Dual Identities makes clear that the tool should facilitate self-reflection, and engagement in self-reflection might help you to cover some of these missing areas. However, ultimately, the tool is designed to focus on dual identity, and it can be used simply and quickly to plot a number based on gut instinct, or it can be used with careful consideration to facilitate self-reflection, thinking, and future planning. Artist-Teacher L felt that the simplicity of the tool meant it does not tell you anything about the person, as used on its own, it does not provide a narrative; however, this is not the function of the tool, instead, it is a tool for personal use. When the Artist-Teacher Likert Scale was used with self-reflection, artist-teachers could use the tool to plot how their identities had moved up and down the continuum over time and to look to the future, in terms of ideal identity.

CONCLUSION

This chapter has outlined the Likert Scale for Dual Identities as a tool to chart current and ideal dual professional identities as well as identity ebbs and flows over time (Steadman, 2023). The tool has been shown to help us understand dual identity, expanding on the idea of dual identity continuums (Daichendt, 2009). The Likert Scale for Dual Identities has been positioned as a tool for self-refection, and the importance of the visual nature of the tool explored. My early use of the tool showed that it has real-world applicability (Nadler, 1980), with artist-teachers easily able to engage with the tool. Early use highlighted the benefits of the tool including its ability to capture flux over different periods and that it is a quick tool to engage with. Limitations of the Likert Scale for Dual Identities were also discussed, including the ten-point scale used in the Artist-Teacher Likert Scale, the static nature of the tool, Likert scales and their link to maths, and its simplistic nature. Ways of overcoming limitations were also shared, including a move toward odd-numbered scales, a tool that encourages continuous documentation, textual anchors, and the importance of accompanying self-refection.

REFERENCES

Bishop, C. (2011) *Artificial hells: Participatory art and the politics of spectatorship*. London: Verso.

Bourdieu, P. (1990) *The logic of practice*. Stanford, CA: Stanford University Press.

Briggs, A. R. J. (2007) 'Exploring professional identities: Middle leadership in further education colleges', *School Leadership and Management*, 27(5), pp. 471–485. doi: 10.1080/13632430701606152.

Cairns, A. (2023a) 'Artist-teacher-researcher-student: Exploring the enterprises of the artist-teacher in adult community learning', *Journal of Research in Post Compulsory Education*, 28(2), pp. 181–206. doi: 10.1080/13596748.2023.2206705.

Cairns, A. (2023b) *Interrogating artist-teacher identity transformation in adult community learning*. Doctoral thesis, Norwich University of the Arts.

Daichendt, G. J. (2009) 'Redefining the artist-teacher', *Journal of Art Education*, 62(5), pp. 33–38. doi: 10.1080/00043125.2009.11519035.

Daichendt, G. J. (2010) *Artist-teacher: A philosophy for creating and teaching*. Bristol: Intellect.

Fejes, A., and Köpsén, S. (2014) 'Vocational teachers' identity formation through boundary crossing', *Journal of Education and Work*, 27(3), pp. 265–283. doi: 10.1080/13639080.2012.742181.

McAdams, D. P. (1993) *The stories we live by: Personal myths and the making of the self*. New York: William Morrow & Co.

Nadler, D. A. (1980) 'Role of models in organisational assessment' in Lawler, E. E., Nadler, D. A., and Canmann, C. (eds) *Organisational assessment, perspectives on the measurement of organisational behaviour and quality of life*. New York: John Wiley and Sons, pp. 25–46.

Parker, T. (2009) 'Continuing the journey - The artist-teacher MA as a catalyst for critical reflection', *International Journal of Art and Design Education*, 28(3), pp. 279–286. doi: 10.1111/j.1476-8070.2009.01623.x.

Steadman, S. (2023) *Identity: Keywords in teacher education*. London: Bloomsbury Academic.

Thornton, A. (2013) *Artist, researcher, teacher: A study of professional identity in art and education*. Chicago: University of Chicago Press.

Wenger, E. (2000) *Communities of practice: Learning meaning and identity*. Cambridge: University of Cambridge Press.

CHAPTER SEVEN

How to use Likert Scales for Dual Identities

> **VIGNETTE: TEACHING/ART**
>
> As an artist-teacher I follow the lead of my artist self. Teaching has felt a lot like an art practice and in the same way I might be given a block of clay, I am given a course. I mould it with my hands. I pull the materials together. I learn the skills I need. I come up with a unique outcome.
>
> Cairns, A. (2022) Teaching/Art. Unpublished vignette.

This chapter outlines a step-by-step guide on creating and using a Likert Scale for Dual Identities.

NAME YOUR IDENTITIES

The first step in creating your Likert Scale for Dual Identities is to name your two most dominant professional identities. You may feel that you have more than two professional identities; however, this tool is specifically for weighing up your FE teacher or trainer identity against your vocational or technical identity. Likert Scales for Dual Identities are ideal for those who are either still practising or are still close to their vocational or technical area and are also to teaching or training in the FE sector.

Identifying your two main identities

You may have a very clear idea of what your two main professional identities are; however, if you are struggling to name these or want extra clarification, engage with one of the techniques listed below: charting experiences and recall qualifications and courses. If you are reading this book there is an assumption that one of these identities will be FE teacher or trainer and that the other will be a vocational or technical area.

Charting experiences: Draw on your past and present experiences of teaching or training and note down the context within FE, whether it be general FE, prison education, community learning, or something else, and the subject(s) you teach or have taught. When identifying your two main professional identities see if there is a subject area that you are repeatedly delivering, this is likely to be one of your two main professional identities, along with your FE teacher or trainer identity.

When charting my experiences, I can reflect on the teaching that I have carried out within an FE context (Table 7.1). I found some of this information on my CV and also discovered that not all subject areas I had taught were listed. Working chronologically, I looked back over my FE teaching career and filled in any gaps.

TABLE 7.1 My charting experiences example

Teaching	Subject
Community workshops	Art
FE 16–19	Art and design level 2
Adult community learning	Art drawing Art drawing and painting Art 3D Art appreciation Life skills Art level 1 Art and design level 2

Recall qualifications and courses: List your qualifications or courses and CPD activities you have previously and are presently engaged in. Identify which of these qualifications and/or courses feel most important to your professional identity. Qualifications are usually well documented on your CV, and you are likely to have fewer overarching qualifications than you do course subjects you teach.

For me, this was quick and easy as my qualifications are well documented on my CV (Table 7.2). Naming other courses and CPD activity was more difficult, and I found that many of these were linked to mandatory training, rather than subject area, and so I decided not to include these.

TABLE 7.2 My recall qualifications and courses example

Qualification	Courses and CPD activity
BA Fine Art	Artist-Teacher in Adult Community Learning Conference
PGCE	*International Journal of Art and Design Education* Conference
MA Fine Art	Association for Research in Post-Compulsory Education Conference
PhD artist-teacher identity formation in adult community learning	Vocational Education and Training Conference

Naming your identities prompt questions

What did I do before I began teaching or training in FE?
What subject area is my vocational or technical training in?
What subject areas am I currently teaching or training in?

PICK A NUMERICAL SCALE

Likert Scales for Dual Identities reply upon a numerical scale. There is no mandatory n-point (number of response points on the scale), used within the Likert Scale for Dual Identities, it is down to you to determine how many points on a scale you feel comfortable working with. However, it is common for Likert scales to have five or seven points, adding more points to the numerical scale can provide a finer degree of measurement and allow you to express a more nuanced opinion. However, with increased options comes the risk of increased confusion and the challenge of distinguishing between closely related response options. If you decide to deviate from the norm of a five- or seven-point numerical scale, it is recommended that you still work with a scale that is based on an odd number, as this will allow you to place yourself directly in the middle of the Likert scale, if necessary. The midpoint will be ideal for those who do not strongly identify as either a teacher or trainer or vocationalist or technicalist or who find both identities to be equally balanced without a leaning towards either.

While the scaling system used within a Likert Scale for Dual Identities is itself numerical, either end of the scale will be attached to a professional identity, your FE teacher or trainer identity at one end and your vocational or technical identity at the other, these endpoints highlight the two extremes of the scale. In interacting with the scale, the closer you place yourself to either extreme, the more you resonate with that professional identity, with each point representing a move closer to either identity. It should be noted that a move closer to either extreme is neither positive nor negative in and of itself, the Likert Scale for Dual Identities is neutral, and neither teaching or trainer nor vocational or technical area is implicitly deemed better or of more or less value than the other. This subjective judgement only comes in when you start to use the scale, depending on your own judgements. This judgement is likely to differ between FE teachers and trainers, and some may value their FE teacher or trainer identity more than their vocational or technical identity, and vice versa, whereas others may value each equally.

Scale and scale anchors

You might find it useful to associate the numerical scale with scale anchors, which provide a textual descriptor for each point, as this helps to provide an extra level of clarity and meaning. The scale should reflect the continuum between teacher or trainer and vocational or technical area, helping visualise the interplay between the two. Five-point and seven-point scale anchors are suggested below; however, if you decide to develop your own scale anchors, ensure that they are unambiguous. Ideally, anchors will be understood by others who share the same vocational or technical area as you.

Five-point scale: For a five-point scale (Table 7.3), scale anchors might be described in the following ways:

TABLE 7.3 Likert Scale for Dual Identities five-point scale example

Vocational/technical area	1	2	3	4	5	Teacher/trainer

1. Teacher/trainer: fully immersed in teaching or trainer pursuits, with minimal emphasis on vocational or technical area.
2. Emerging educator: prioritises teaching or trainer, while still engaging in vocational or technical activities.
3. Balanced practitioner: achieves a harmonious balance between teaching or training and vocational or technical pursuits.
4. Vocational/technical instructor: prioritises their vocational or technical area while still engaging in educational activities.
5. Vocationalist/technicalist: fully immersed in vocational or technical pursuits, with minimal emphasis on teaching or training.

Seven-point scale: For a seven-point scale (Table 7.4), scale anchors might be described in the following ways:

TABLE 7.4 Likert Scale for Dual Identities seven-point scale example

Vocational/technical area	1	2	3	4	5	6	7	Teacher/trainer

1. Teacher/trainer: fully immersed in teaching or training pursuits, with minimal emphasis on vocational or technical area.
2. Focused teacher/trainer: a significant amount of your role is focused on formal education.
3. Emerging educator: prioritises teaching or training while still engaging in vocational or technical activities.
4. Balanced practitioner: achieves a harmonious balance between teaching or training and vocational or technical pursuits.
5. Vocational/technical instructor: prioritises vocational or technical area while still engaging in educational activities.
6. Focused vocationalist/technicalist: a significant amount of your role is focused on your vocational or technical area.
7. Vocationalist/technicalist: fully immersed in vocational or technical pursuits, with minimal emphasis on teaching or training.

Larger scales: For numerical scales with 9 points or more, you may find attaching scale anchors difficult due to the nuance required in their wording. However, you might find it useful to have more variations to choose from when placing yourself numerically.

Pick a numerical scale prompt questions

Would a five-point or seven-point scale work best for you?
Would you better interact with a scale that has scale anchors attached to it or a scale that is just numerical?
What factors or considerations are most relevant to your decision when placing yourself on the scale?

PICK A COLOUR SCHEME

Colour scheme in Likert Scales for Dual Identities emerged when I was engaging in research into artist-teachers using an early version of the scales presented in the previous chapter. In his work on artist-teachers, Alan Thornton (2013) asserted that teachers were blue, artists were red, and artist-teachers were purple, giving a clear colour scheme to base the Artist-Teacher Likert Scale on. This section expands on these ideas.

Using a colour scheme helps to make the Likert Scale for Dual Identities more visually engaging. However, there are no set rules for which vocations are which colour, as this is open to interpretation; members of the same vocational or technical area may conceptualise this differently. This is legitimate, as you are building your own scale and the choices you make must be meaningful to you, alone. Similarly, you might wish to change the colour of the teacher or trainer, if blue does not feel fitting for you, and if you are an artist, you may wish to replace the colour red with another colour which feels more suitable to you.

It should be noted that your colour choices will be abstract and subjective, they might be based on how you feel about teaching or trainer and your vocational or technical area and the colours that come to mind when you consider them. It might simply be that you pick your two favourite colours from the colour wheel and proceed that way. To help you make this choice, colours and their generally agreed symbolic meaning are listed below.

Colour scheme

In picking a colour scheme the goal is to encourage self-reflection and individual expression. For simplicity I have focused on primary (red, blue, and yellow) and secondary (orange, green, and purple) colours and their meanings, it is worth noting that colour meanings may differ across different cultural contexts. In loose terms we tend to read these colours in the following ways in the UK:

Red: Red is usually associated with passion, love, energy, warmth, and power.
Blue: Blue can represent calmness, stability, trust, and serenity.
Yellow: Yellow is generally associated with happiness, optimism, energy, and warmth.
Orange: Orange often symbolises enthusiasm, creativity, energy, and warmth.
Green: Green typically symbolises nature, growth, harmony, and freshness.
Purple: Purple commonly represents luxury, royalty, mystery, spirituality, creativity, and sophistication.

COLOURED SCALE EXAMPLES

Artist-teacher (red and blue)

The use of red for an artist might represent the passion the individual has for the subject, while the use of blue for the teacher might denote the stability they feel it comes with the role.

Musician-trainer (orange and green)

The use of orange might symbolise the creative nature of being a musician, while the use of green might represent growth into a new identity as a trainer.

Florist-teacher (green and yellow)

For a florist, green might represent nature, reflecting a practical and central part of their practice, while yellow might symbolise the warmth they feel towards teaching.

Pick a colour scheme prompt questions

What colour do you think of when you think of FE teaching or training?
What colour comes to mind when reflecting on your vocational or technical area?
Are there colours you feel drawn to or repelled by?
If you had to express your current role through a colour, what would it be?
Are there specific memories or experiences in your life that are connected to certain colours?
What emotions or feelings do you associate with certain roles, how does this relate to these colours?

PLACEMENT

Placement is a key component of using Likert Scales for Dual Identities, in placing yourself on the scale you create, you will be effectively measuring your own attitudes, options, and perceptions of your dual professional identity. When placing yourself it is best to try and avoid ambiguity, always be clear from what position you are placing yourself and consider that you are placing yourself to indicate your current identity.

Five positions

There are five positions from which you can place yourself on a Likert Scale for Dual Identities – me, FE teacher or trainer colleagues, learners, vocational or technical colleagues, and wider world – and each position is outlined below. When placing yourself you might consider one position or each position in turn:

ME: How do you view your professional identity?

FE TEACHER OR TRAINER COLLEAGUES: How do your colleagues within an FE context view your professional identity?

LEARNERS:	How do your FE learners consider your professional identity?
VOCATIONAL OR TECHNICAL COLLEAGUES:	How do your vocational or technical colleagues view your professional identity?
WIDER WORLD:	How does everyone else view your professional identity?

By switching positions, you can use the Likert Scale for Dual Identities to explore your professional identity from multiple angles and consider the viewpoints of others. In this activity, you might simply consider the viewpoints of others (FE teacher or trainer colleagues, learners, vocational or technical colleagues, and people from your wider world) or you may ask others to place you. Asking others to place you on your Likert Scale for Dual Identities can be beneficial, as there may be some things about yourself that are known by others but not by you. This can help you foster a more comprehensive understanding of your professional identity and make judgements on whether you are happy with how others view you or if you wish to change how you are viewed by them. Additionally, it may be difficult to make judgements on how others view you, without direct feedback from them. You can also use the 'me' position to place yourself based on your own judgements of your professional identity; this is likely to be the most common use of a Likert Scale for Dual Identities.

Factors

Factors in this context are things that might impact your placement on your Likert Scale for Dual Identities. When placing yourself consider the following eight factors: understanding the position, context, consistency, honesty, experience, temporal considerations, extreme responses, and applicability.

Understanding the position: Ensure that you fully understand the position you are placing yourself from.

Context: Consider the context of where you are when placing yourself on the scale. Try to complete the scale in a neutral context, as if you place yourself on the scale; while in your teaching or training environment or vocational or technical enviroment, this might impact where you place yourself on the scale.

Consistency: Reflect on your responses to ensure consistency and consider when you are placing yourself on the scale and if you should place yourself in a consistent way, such as always on Monday at 3pm.

Honesty: Provide honest and genuine responses. Your authentic input is key for the tool to work and be impactful on your professional identity.

Experience: Think about your recent experiences and how relevant these are to FE teaching or training and your vocational or technical area.

Temporal considerations: Consider whether your response might change based on time or circumstances. Some attitudes or opinions may vary depending on when you are asked. Remember that Likert Scales for Dual Identities draw on nowness and are focused on reflecting the moment.

Extreme responses: While extreme responses are sometimes warranted (placing yourself at either end of your scale), be cautious about using them excessively. You might find that responses are more extreme after intense experiences, such as after a particularly good or bad day. Moderation in responses can lead to a more nuanced understanding of your professional identity over time.

Applicability: Consider how applicable each professional identity is to you currently.

Placement prompt questions

What position would be most useful for you to use?
How do you see yourself?
How easy is it to judge how others see you?
Do you have an idea of how you want others to see you?
What control do you have over how others see you?

USAGE AND AVERAGES

The next step in creating your Likert Scale for Dual Identities is to consider how frequently you will use the scale. This relates to how often you will use it and goes on to include how you can draw averages from usages to build a picture of your professional identity from any of the five positions: me, FE teacher or trainer colleagues, learners, vocational or technical colleagues, and wider world. The usefulness of your Likert Scale for Dual Identities will grow each time you use it, and long-term use is ideal and recommended. Continue to chart your current professional identity as your career progresses to create a visual representation of who you are professionally over time.

Timeframes

I have suggested five timeframes to use the Likert Scale for Dual Identities within: yearly, six monthly, monthly, weekly, daily, and as-and-when. You should pick the timeframe that will be most beneficial to you and your professional identity.

Yearly: Placing yourself yearly will require deep refection on the year just gone (Figure 7.1). You might decide to place yourself every new year or every

HOW TO USE LIKERT SCALES FOR DUAL IDENTITIES

new academic year. This timeframe is based on an average placement over the year. Looking backwards when completing this task can be difficult, as the Likert Scale for Dual Identities is intended to be used as a tool to assess and reflect current identities. While you may try to look back two or more years to chart your identities, the tool is better used from the stance of the current day.

Position: Me						
Ideal			x			
Artist	1	2	3	4	5	Teacher
2022 2023 2024				x x	 x 	

FIGURE 7.1 My yearly Likert Scale for Dual Identities example.

Six monthly: Placing yourself every six months will allow you to keep on top of your changing professional identity (Figure 7.2). You may choose January and June, or another six-monthly period, this timeframe will require you to place yourself based on an average of the chosen six months.

Position: Me						
Ideal			x			
Artist	1	2	3	4	5	Teacher
Jan 23 Jun 23 Jan 24 Jun 24				x x 	 x x	

FIGURE 7.2 My six-monthly Likert Scale for Dual Identities example.

Monthly: Placing yourself every month will provide a good overview of your professional identity over time (Figure 7.3). Pick a time in the month to sit down, reflect and place yourself on the Likert Scale for Dual Identities, the end of the month is recommended as this will allow you to reflect clearly on everything that has happened. You will need to consider your identity over the month and how you felt about your identity over this period before placing yourself.

Position: Me						
Ideal			x			
Artist	1	2	3	4	5	Teacher
Jan				x		
Feb		x				
Mar				x		
Apr		x				
May				x		
Jun				x		
Jul	x					
Aug	x					
Sept			x			
Oct				x		
Nov				x		
Dec			x			

FIGURE 7.3 My monthly Likert Scale for Dual Identities example.

Weekly: Placing yourself weekly will give you an in-depth look at real-time changes to your professional identity (Figure 7.4). Pick a time in the week to sit down, reflect and place yourself on the Likert Scale for Dual Identities, this might be any day of the week, but the end of the week is recommended as this will allow you to reflect clearly on the last seven days.

Position: Me						
Ideal			x			
Artist	1	2	3	4	5	Teacher
01/01/24				x		
08/01/34			x			
15/01/24				x		
22/01/24				x		

FIGURE 7.4 My weekly Likert Scale for Dual Identities example.

Daily: Placing yourself daily will allow you to track and chart your professional identity and is ideal for those who are questioning their changing professional identity (Figure 7.5). Spend time at the end of each day to place yourself based on the day's activities.

HOW TO USE LIKERT SCALES FOR DUAL IDENTITIES

Position: Me						
Ideal			x			
Artist	1	2	3	4	5	Teacher
1st				x		
2nd					x	
3rd		x				
4th				x		
5th		x				
6th		x				
7th		x				

FIGURE 7.5 My daily Likert Scale for Dual Identities example.

As-and-when: Place yourself as regularly as you feel necessary (Figure 7.6), this might be multiple times a day or week, or as-and-when you find yourself considering your professional identity. Regular use of the Likert Scale of Dual Identities is recommended, as this is when the tool is most accurate and the results most useful.

Position: Me						
Ideal			x			
Artist	1	2	3	4	5	Teacher
1st AM				x		
1st PM			x			
3rd EVE		x				

FIGURE 7.6 My as-and-when Likert Scale for Dual Identities example.

Usage and averages prompt questions

How often do you consider your professional identity?
Do you consider your professional identity too little or too often?
How often would it be useful to consider your professional identity?

REFLECTION

To make the most of Likert Scales for Dual Identities your engagement should go beyond placing yourself on the scale, and you must also reflect on where you have placed yourself. You should consider if you are happy with where you are on the scale or if you want to move in either direction. This act will allow you to use the Likert Scale for Dual Identities to aid personal growth and provide insights into your evolving perspectives on your FE teacher or trainer and vocational or technical identities.

Engagement in self-reflection on your Likert Scale for Dual Identities works with the five positions outlined: me, FE teacher or trainer colleagues, learners, vocational or technical colleagues, and the wider world. You will either be reflecting on your own ideal identity through the 'me' position or you on how you would ideally like to be seen professionally by others (Figures 7.7 and 7.8). It should be noted that you might want to be viewed differently by each of the outlined groups, as you find that your professional identity shifts with the context you find yourself in, or equally you might want to be seen in the same way across each group, both options are valid and down to personal preference.

Position: Me						
Ideal			x			
Artist	1	2	3	4	5	Teacher
Current				x		

FIGURE 7.7 My current and ideal identity Likert Scale for Dual Identities example, from the 'me' position.

Position: Learners						
Ideal			x			
Artist	1	2	3	4	5	Teacher
Current					x	

FIGURE 7.8 My current and ideal identity Likert Scale for Dual Identities example, from the 'learner' position.

Analysing Likert Scale for Dual Identity data

The numerical scales used within the Likert Scale for Dual Identities provide you with a quantitative reference point for your professional identity. However, you might find that the real value comes from the self-reflection and discussions with others that arise during and after the scaling process and how the Likert Scale for Dual Identities can impact how you view and transform your professional identity. Analysis of your Likert Scale for Dual Identities might reveal truths related to ebbs and flows in your professional identity. This can be true for yearly, monthly, weekly, daily, and, to a degree, as-and-when use. What the analysis tells you about your identity might vary between time frames.

Yearly: Analysis of a yearly Likert Scale for Dual Identities may glean how your professional identity shifts as your professional career continues. This can be particularly useful for those new to teaching or training in FE or those still studying. Year-on-year you will be able to reflect on your overarching identity as a vocational or technical FE teacher or trainer. You may note shifts from your pre-service identity, to your first year in the sector, and beyond.

Monthly: Analysis of a monthly Likert Scale for Dual Identities will reflect how the nature of an academic year impacts your professional identity. You may come across trends related to times of the year and how you identify professionally.

Weekly: Analysis of a weekly Likert Scale for Dual Identities works in a similar way to monthly analysis. This option will offer a more nuanced look and may be more reflective of your professional identity as you will collect more data on yourself and your professional identity.

Daily: Analysis of a daily Likert Scale for Dual Identities builds on the weekly analysis option and provides even more data to be reflected upon. This might be particularly useful if you find how you spend your week is split between FE teaching or training and your vocational or vocational work, as you can assess each day individually.

As-and-when: Analysis of an as-and-when Likert Scale for Dual Identities is likely to be more difficult as there will be no structure to the data collected. However, looking closely at the data may help you decipher patterns.

Visual and numerical analysis

These two techniques should yield the same results, which you use is down to personal preference. Before you begin you will want to consider if you work better with visual representations or numbers.

Visual analysis: Likert Scales for Dual Identities can be analysed visually, and with a quick look you will be able to identify where you are on the scale and where you want to be on the scale. The use of colour helps here, as it will be easy to see if any change has taken place, or how far you must move in either direction to meet your ideal professional identity. For a more impactful visual, you may consider only colouring in the space on the Likert Scale for Dual Identities where your current identity sits.

When visually analysing my Likert Scale for Dual Identities I use the colour coding as a quick way to check where I am (Figure 7.9). As the colours build over time, I can create a useful chart of my changing professional identity.

Position: Me						
Ideal			x			
Artist	1	2	3	4	5	**Teacher**
01/01/24				x		
08/01/24		x				
15/01/24				x		
22/01/24				x		

FIGURE 7.9 My Likert Scale for Dual Identities visual analysis example.

Numerical analysis: Likert Sales for Dual Identities provide numerical data that can be used to work out your average professional identity over time. Data from yearly, six monthly, monthly, daily, and as-and-when Likert Scales for Dual Identities work particularly well here. Simply add your positional numbers up and divide by the number of Likert Scales for Dual Identities you have completed, and this will give you your average professional identity over time.

With numerical analysis, you can look for trends, and you might note the range of different positions you have held on your Likert Scale for Dual Identities. If the range is large and you find your professional identity moving from one extreme to another this might suggest a professional identity in flux, or conversely, you might find that your professional identity is consistent over time. Neither of these options are better than the other, this judgement is down to personal preference, you may prefer to identify more strongly as a teacher or trainer in an education setting, more of a vocationalist or technicalist in another setting, or you may prefer to have a consistent identity regardless of context. It will be useful to reflect on this and which works best for you. Additionally, you might find it useful to consider your most common identity placement and why this is so. This could be directly related to how much time you are spending in certain contexts or be impacted by another factor.

When using numerical analysis, the first thing I look for is my average identity over time. I believe that this is the most impactful piece of data I can take from my Likert Scale for Dual Identities as it allows me to compare my average current identity over time to my current ideal identity. I have used Figure 7.10 to document this analysis, and the mode and range are also documented. I can see that I have not met my ideal identity of 3 yet and can use these results as a catalyst for change, before checking back in, in six months to see if my average identity has shifted.

Position: Me							
Ideal				x			
Artist	1	2	3	4	5		Teacher
01/01/23				x			4
01/06/23			x				3
01/01/24				x			4
01/06/24				x			4
	Mode: 4		Range: 3-4		Average (4+3+4+4)/4		3.75

FIGURE 7.10 My Likert Scale for Dual Identities numerical analysis example.

Reflection prompt questions

Do you work best with visual or numerical prompts for reflection?
How often will you find time to reflect on your professional identity?
How will you remind yourself to engage with self-reflection?
Will you reflect on your own or engage in discussions with others?

FUTURE PLANNING

Use the Likert Scale for Dual Identities to assess and evaluate your progress towards maintaining or achieving your ideal professional identity. To do this you must consider your identity goals and any challenges you might face in reaching them. Future planning with a Likert Scale for Dual Identities is intended to encourage and support self-reflection. The numerical scale, colour coding system, and optional textual anchors help to facilitate goal clarity. Additionally, the use of the tool adds a layer of accountability, helping you to take proactive steps towards positive change, in either direction on your Likert Scale for Dual Identities, whether you want to move further towards your FE teacher or trainer identity, or your vocational or technical identity, or find yourself in the middle of the two.

Within the reflection stage, you should have already placed your ideal identity. It is key to continue to revisit your ideal professional identity, as this is just as likely to change over time as your current identity is. What is ideal now, may not be ideal in one, five, or ten years – or possibly even sooner. You must continue to consider your current ideal identity as this will guide your future planning. Once you have placed your ideal identity be SMART and consider:

Specific: If you have been specific about your ideal identity and if you have tied it to a scale point and anchor.

Measurable: If you have decided how often will you check in with your ideal identity and progress you are making towards it.

Achievable: If you have given yourself adequate time to reach your ideal identity and if you can make necessary changes, for example, in how you spend your time or which CPD activities you can access.

Realistic: If you can take the actions required to reach your current ideal identity and if you have the resources to do so.

Time based: If you have set yourself a review date and put in place a structure to remind yourself to check in on your progress, for example, putting a reminder in your diary.

Future planning prompt questions

How close are you to your ideal identity?
What changes do you need to make to reach your ideal identity?
What changes will happen if you reach your ideal identity?
Has this always been your ideal identity?
Is your ideal identity likely to change in one, three, or five years?

> ### *TRY THIS!* CREATE YOUR LIKERT SCALE FOR DUAL IDENTITIES
>
> You are now ready to create your own Likert Scale for Dual Identities, by bringing together your two main professional identities, numerical scale, colour scheme, and position. Work in a basic Likert Scale created digitally, or draw the scale by hand, plot your numerical scale along the Likert scale, and place one of your professional identities at either end. Colour the scale in according to your selections, and reflect on your current position and plot yourself, then reflect on your ideal position and plot this too. Make a note of the date you set these positions, as this will be a useful reminder when revisiting your Likert Scale for Dual Identities to check your progress or plot new positions. Depending on how often you plan to engage with the Likert Scale for Dual Identities, it can be useful to add reminders into your diary or planner.
>
> When putting my Likert Scale for Dual Identities together I decided to focus on my artist and teacher identities, as these felt like the two main identities that I embody. I have kept to Thornton's (2013) colour suggestions for artist (red) and teachers (blue), as I have been working with these for so long that it felt strange to change them now! I tend to check in with my Likert Scale for Dual Identities weekly, as I feel this helps catch the ebbs and flows best for me. I choose to engage in the 'me' position, as this is the position that helps me best juggle the two identities in a way that I am happy with.

Create your own Likert Scale for Dual Identities prompt questions

Are these definitely my two main professional identities?
Is the scale working?
Have I chosen the most appropriate colours?
Have I chosen the right position to place myself from?
Have I been honest in my placement on the scale?

REFERENCE

Thornton, A. (2013) *Artist, researcher, teacher: A study of professional identity in art and education.* Chicago: University of Chicago Press.

CHAPTER EIGHT

From use to insight
FE teacher and trainers' reflections on Likert Scales for Dual Identities

---

VIGNETTE: FRIENDSHIP

Are you telling me what I want to hear, or are you telling me the truth?
Cairns, A. (2022) Friendship. Unpublished vignette.

INTRODUCTION

In this chapter, reflections from FE teachers and trainers are shared; the purpose of this chapter is to highlight the use of Likert Scales for Dual Identities by practitioners in the sector. Their experience is intended to help you better understand and negotiate your use of the tool and the techniques used within it. For each technique, the benefits, limitations, ease of use, and impact on professional identity are explored. The FE teachers and trainers drawn upon in this chapter were recruited to take part via an online open call for FE teachers and trainers across social media platforms. Their participation was voluntary. Each FE teacher and trainer quoted in this chapter has given permission for their experience, and name to be shared to help situate the tool in real life.

Before we begin, let me introduce you to the FE teachers and trainers who have been testing Likert Scales for Dual Identities: Joyce I-Hui Chen, Ronnie Houselander-Cook, and Sue Chillingworth.

NAMING YOUR DUAL IDENTITY

The FE teachers and trainers who engaged with the Likert Scales for Dual Identities were introduced to naming your dual identity as a stage aimed towards helping you to name your two most dominant professional identities. It was outlined that, while they might feel they have more than two professional identities, this tool is specifically for weighing up FE teacher or trainer identity against vocational or technical identity.

FE teachers and trainers were introduced to the two techniques for naming their two most dominant professional identities, to be used at either end of their Likert Scale for Dual Identities: charting experiences and recall qualifications and courses. FE teachers and trainers were initially asked to pick one technique, but many felt that both the techniques would work together. The extract below outlines Sue's interaction with this stage of the tool.

> It makes you think about how you're spending your time... just seeing it actually helps.
> - Sue

For Sue, naming her two professional identities acted as a self-reflection activity. It allowed her the space to consider and better understand how she had allocated her time and energy between her two professional identities. Sue found the visual nature of the Likert Scale for Dual Identities to be powerful, as her identities become easier to comprehend and more tangible. FE teachers and trainers were inclined to use both techniques for naming identities, suggesting that each offered them a unique insight that, when combined, gave a fuller picture of their dual identities. FE teachers and trainers who have engaged with the tool found this stage to be beneficial, and Ronnie stated that naming her two professional identities gave her more agency and authority over who she is. Ronnie also added that it is helpful when communicating her identities to others. The limitations of this stage centred around it focusing on just two professional identities.

> I suppose the limitations are that you've only got two [identities]... coming together. Some people might want to break that up even further, like for myself.
> - Sue

For Sue and Joyce, the dual nature of the Likert Scale for Dual Identities was limiting, as it restricted them to considering only two dominant professional identities. Sue found that the complexity of her professional identity was not adequately captured. However, the tool had a clear impact on FE teachers and trainers' professional identities, making them consider what they do, how they spend their time, and why. For others who engaged with the tool, it allowed them to take a comprehensive look at their career trajectories and the professional identities they have inhabited. The tool helped them to clarify their professional purpose and was effective in aiding identity and affirming core professional passions and strengths. The Likert Scale for Dual Identities provided FE teachers and trainers with a sense of validation and reaffirmation of their professional identities, and their interactions with the tool showed that it had both an emotional and cognitive impact, increased their confidence around identity, and helped to informed decisions about their careers.

PICKING A NUMERICAL SCALE

Next, FE teachers and trainers were introduced to the scaling element of Likert Scales for Dual Identities. It was outlined that the tool relies upon a numerical scale and FE teachers and trainers were introduced to the different scales: 5-point scales, 7-point scales, and larger scales (9-point scales, 11-point scales, 13-point scales, and 15-point scales). FE teachers and trainers were also introduced to the scale anchors, which provided textual descriptors for numerical points. The extract below outlines Ronnie and Joyce's interaction with this stage.

> I think a benefit is that I'm quite indecisive, so it's quite nice to actually have a definition with a number and be like 'OK, that.'.
>
> - Ronnie

For Ronnie, the main benefit of the numerical scale and textual anchors being presented together was the impact this had on her ability to make a choice, as together they allowed her to quantify her feelings numerically, while also providing her with clarity. The numerical scales offered Ronnie a straightforward way to express her position without having to overthink it. Ronnie had a preference for concrete, well-defined choices that the Likert Scale for Dual Identities offered. However, she felt a limitation of this stage was the difficulty in capturing the movement of identity flux, which impacted on how easy she felt the tool was to engage with. Other FE teachers and trainers who engaged in the tool found using the scale to be difficult due to the fluxuating nature of their professional careers and thus identities. However, they were reminded that the placement on the scale reflects their current identity, and FE teachers and trainers continued to find it difficult to consider a single point in time. Once selected, the impact of picking a numerical scale for professional identity, and engaging with it, was clear, with FE teachers and trainers noting that engagement revealed things to them about how they see themselves and what they are happy with in terms of their professional identities.

FE teachers and trainers who have engaged with the tool found placing themselves on the scale allowed for deep self-reflection and development of self-awareness of both their career and professional identity. For these FE teachers and trainers, the tool was effective in encouraging introspection and self-assessment, the tool prompted them to think about their professional journey and future direction, going beyond superficial assessments. They shared that the tool provided a structured opportunity for self-reflection, which might otherwise be overlooked in the busyness of daily life and mitigated against drifting in their career paths. The most selected scales by FE teachers and trainers who have engaged with the tool were the small five- and seven-point scales, and it was felt that these allowed for enough nuance without becoming too difficult to handle. Joyce felt the larger the scale, the more complicated the task became. FE teachers and trainers were able to use their self-reflection to select the scale that was most appropriate for them.

> I don't think there's a lot of limitations about using the scale... as you make it very clear what... one means, what... five means.
>
> - Joyce

Joyce shared that for her, the clarity of the tool is the most beneficial aspect of it, with the numerical scale and accompanying textual anchors giving her a clear understanding of what each point of the scale represented. The one limitation outlined by Joyce focuses on the linguistic used within the textual anchors, and Joyce suggested that the appropriateness of the terms used may depend on how each FE teacher and trainer views themself.

PICKING A COLOUR SCHEME

FE teachers and trainers were introduced to colour schemes as a mechanism to make the tool more visually engaging. It was outlined that there are no set rules for which colour is selected for the role of teacher or trainer or for vocational or technical area and that colours and colour schemes are open to interpretation. FE teachers and trainers were asked to reflect on what colour their FE teacher or trainer identity is and what colour their vocational or technical identity is. Colours introduced to FE teachers and trainers included red, blue, yellow, orange, green, and purple. The extracts below outline Ronnie, Joyce, and Sue's interaction with this stage.

> I kind of feel like an orange-yellow, because I don't think [teaching] is always happiness, but I think it is always enthusiasm. But I feel like you can't be a good teacher unless you're optimistic.
>
> - Ronnie

> I love colours... I actually quite like thinking about teacher identity as green.
>
> - Joyce

Ronnie and Joyce were able to engage in the interpretative nature of the colour scheme stage of the Likert Scale for Dual Identities and easily resonated with the colours and descriptors given, and they both explored their professional identities through the symbolic meanings of colour. Ronnie felt that the inclusion of descriptors allowed her to consider the attributes of her professional identities and how they align with certain colours. Ronnie and Joyce's differing colour selections for the same professional identity of 'teacher' highlights the personal choice within this stage of the Likert Scale for Dual Identities and how this choice is open to interpretation. Ronnie felt that the given descriptors were accurate and said everything she needed them to say, in relation to how she viewed the professional identity she was attributing to it.

> The benefit is it gets you thinking about descriptive terms of how you would describe your identity. I think when you look at the colour combined with a descriptive term you... contextualise [it] with how you're feeling about your practice... it's just less abstract.
>
> - Ronnie

For Ronnie, picking a colour scheme facilitated reflective thinking and prompted her to think in descriptive terms about her professional identities. Ronnie found that the combination of colours with descriptive terms made it easier to contextualise her professional identities and made abstract concepts more concrete and provided a more holistic understanding of her professional identities. The stage also enhanced her self-awareness and provided a tangible way to explore, understand, and articulate her dual professional identity.

Some limitations came to light from teachers and trainers who had engaged with the tool; Ronnie felt some colours were missing, namely pink, while Joyce considered the implications for those with colour blindness, and Sue picked up on colour and cultural differences.

> [W]ith colours... it depends on what part of the world you're living and your culture and your beliefs and all those kind of things as well.
>
> - Sue

Sue acknowledged, as the book does, that colour meanings can vary depending on cultural context, location, and personal beliefs. Sue was able to engage with the tool based on her own interpretations of colours, and the engagement in the tool by FE teachers and trainers showed this stage to be inclusive and flexible. FE teachers and trainers were able to bring their own cultural and personal experiences into their reflections, making the activity more relevant and meaningful to everyone.

The ease of this stage differed for each FE teacher and trainer who engaged with the tool. Ronnie felt that the task maybe more intuitive for visually oriented individuals who can easily make connections between feelings and colours and felt that those without a strong visual preference or prior knowledge of colour theory might find the exercise more abstract. However, for Ronnie, this was a straightforward and immediate task that facilitated a deeper and quicker reflective process. Other FE teachers and trainers suggested that colour choices might change over time, reflecting the dynamic aspect of professional identity and the value of this reflective process. Those who have engaged in the tool highlighted the value of periodically revisiting their Likert Scale for Dual Identities and updating it to capture the evolving nature of their professional experiences and feelings, allowing FE teachers and trainers to reassess and modify their colour associations as their emotions and experiences shift. These reflections suggest that the tool is seen as adaptable and as promoting a more realistic and holistic understanding of professional identity, fostering a comprehensive self-awareness.

PLACING YOURSELF

FE teachers and trainers were introduced to placing themselves on their Likert Scale for Dual Identities, as a key component of using the tool. This stage was outlined to FE teachers and trainers as an effective way of measuring their attitudes, options, and perceptions of their professional identity, and they were encouraged to place their current and ideal identities on the scale. FE teachers and trainers were given five positions to place themselves from the 'me' position or from the position of others including FE teacher and trainer colleagues, learners, vocational and technical colleagues, or the wider world. The extract below outlines Sue and Joyce's interaction with this technique.

> I think all of them, if I'm honest. Can I have all of them?
> - Sue

Both Sue and Joyce expressed a desire to engage with all outlined positions used with the Likert Scale for Dual Identities. They suggested that it would be beneficial to see themselves from multiple perspectives, rather than from a singular viewpoint, as they understood the importance of various perspectives to fully understand their dual professional identities. For them, the benefits of engaging with the lenses and placing themselves on the Likert Scale for Dual Identities include its reflective properties.

> It makes you personally think and reflect on what you're doing. It's useful for other people to see how you're working.
>
> - Sue

For Sue, the tool prompted self-reflection on her professional identities. Within this refection she considered how her professional identities aligned with her own attitudes, options, and perceptions of the identities more widely. Sue found this encouraged self-awareness and introspection. Additionally, Sue felt that the tool allowed for others to see how she is working and identifying, facilitating transparency and communication among colleagues, providing a way to share and discuss professional identities, and potentially helping to foster a collaborative environment. In this way, Sue found that the tool could contribute to her professional growth and development, allowing her to identify areas for improvement and professional learning.

The ease of this stage seemed to be related to the chosen position, with those working with the 'me' position finding it easy to place themselves, while those working with other positions, such as the wider world or colleagues, finding it much harder. FE teachers and trainers who engaged with the colleague position found it difficult to accurately assess how their colleagues perceived them, outlining this as a complex and subjective task, made harder without substantial interaction and feedback from colleagues themselves. They felt that to understand their colleagues' perceptions of them would require significant time spent together and regular interactions; without this, they believed they risked ineffectiveness in capturing a true reflection from this position.

Placing yourself had a clear impact on professional identity for FE teachers and trainers who have engaged with the tool. Joyce outlined that this allowed for self-exploration and made her think about and analyse who she was. In this way, Joyce found the tool useful for prompting self-reflection and identifying changes she needed to make to her professional identity. Joyce was also able to consider ways to align her professional identities with her values and goals which allowed her to maintain a sense of purpose and fulfilment and mitigate feelings of disillusionment. As well as placing her current identity, Joyce engaged with placing her ideal identity.

> I think [the Likert Scale for Dual Identities] could be a really good reflective tool... you can use it to think about your ideal self... in the future...

and how to get there... that would be useful and again visualising it helps.

— Joyce

Joyce found that this use of the tool facilitated valuable self-reflection and self-assessment that helped her to recognise areas for professional development. For Joyce, this promoted future-oriented thinking around long-term goals and aspirations and an important aspect of this for Joyce was the ability to use the Likert Scale for Dual Identities to visualise her position on the scale, which made abstract concepts more concrete and enhanced understanding. Joyce also found this stage to serve as a motivational device that allowed her to consider and set clear, achievable goals.

USAGE AND AVERAGES

FE teachers and trainers were introduced to usage and averages as a way of building a picture of dual professional identity from any of the five positions in the previous stage. FE teachers and trainers were introduced to the six usage timeframes, including yearly, six monthly, monthly, weekly, daily, and as-and-when. The extract below outlines Ronnie's interaction with this technique, with a focus on using the tool monthly.

> The benefit would be that... you can almost capture the beginning, middle and ends of cycles of events, opportunities, situations which is quite nice because how you resolve and interact and be in those will influence how you feel [and] how you perceive yourself through your actions.
>
> — Ronnie

Ronnie shared that she would engage with the Likert Scale for Dual Identities monthly as she felt this would allow her to compare months to each other and see how each month leads on from the last. Ronnie also felt that this timeframe was large enough to allow her to capture the beginning, middle, and end of various cycles, such as the start, middle, and end of an academic year. However, despite this, Ronnie does question if a monthly timeframe would produce an accurate reflection of the year. Ronnie felt that this usage would facilitate self-reflection on actions and interactions over different periods, which would help to shed light on how she sees herself in different roles over time and provide insights into how she adapts to changing circumstances. For Ronnie, the tool has a focus on professional development, as it allowed her to identify areas of strength and opportunities for growth, thereby enhancing her professional identity. Joyce also considered usage and suggested that the timeframe chosen needs to be regular but long enough for there to have been differences. For Joyce, this would be every three months. Sue stated she would engage every six months, while other FE teachers and trainers, like Ronnie, suggested that monthly would suit their schedules best. And some stated they would have liked to use the tool weekly but felt this would be unrealistic due to time constraints. Ronnie felt that if the Likert Scale for Dual Identities was engaged with as-and-when, the results would be too emotionally driven, as she might only place herself on a really good or bad days. Differing engagement by FE teachers and trainers showed how the tool can be used to fit different rhythms and commitments that align to each individual. FE teachers and trainers commented on how dual professional identity is influenced by the nature and frequency of the tasks they undertook in each professional identity they hold and how the Likert Scale for Dual Identities fits into this.

FE teachers and trainers felt that this stage would impact their professional identity, as it would help them to actively change their professional identities and help them to maintain a balance between their two professional identities. Those who have engaged with the tool suggested that this would happen by using the Likert Scale for Dual Identities to review their time commitments to each and to guide them in allocating time more effectively to ensure neither is neglected.

REFLECTION

FE teachers and trainers were introduced to reflecting with the Likert Scale for Dual Identities as a way to make the most out of the tool, and that their engagement in the tool should go beyond placing themself on the scale. Five different time scales for refection were suggested: yearly, monthly, weekly, daily, and as-and-when. The extract below outlines Ronnie and Sue's interaction with this technique. FE teachers and trainers who have engaged in the tool were enthusiastic about the visual nature of the tool and the ability to see their reflections over time. Sue felt this was beneficial to the Likert Scale for Dual Identities as an evaluation tool, which could significantly enhance her reflective practice. FE teachers and trainers noted that the tool could aid in tracking and analysing changes or trends in their dual identities as they were able to observe patterns, identify shifts, and gain insights into their professional development and professional identity over time.

> It feels like quite a nice concise way of reflecting actually, because sometimes with reflection there's like an 8,000,000 step cycle... It's just nice to think about it without having to think 'how am I going to improve'... it's not about improving... [it's] sort of [about] tracking something instead.
>
> - Ronnie

Ronnie and Sue both appreciated the simplicity and directness of the Likert Scale for Dual Identities as a tool for reflection and found it easy to engage with. For Ronnie, the tool was a straightforward and efficient way to reflect, and she particularly appreciated the emphasis on tracking rather than on improvement. Ronnie felt she could use the tool to monitor and understand her dual identities over time, rather than immediately seeking ways to change her professional identity. For Ronnie these aspects reduced the pressure that she often associates with reflective practices, making reflection more accessible and less daunting and in turn encouraging her to engage in regular and honest self-assessment. Other FE teachers and trainers who have engaged with the tool also found how easily and quickly they could place themselves on the scale without feeling overwhelmed by the process.

> [It] makes you think about... how you're working as a professional artist or photographer. [You] reflect on where you're going and if are you on the right track to be getting there. Really, I suppose... it's down to goals, isn't it?... It would help you reflect [and] set your long-term goals as well as your short-term goals.
>
> - Sue

For Sue, the impact of reflection with her Likert Scale for Dual Identities on her professional identity was related to goal setting and understanding her current position and future direction in her career. Reflecting in this way, Sue can adjust her strategies and efforts to stay on the right track, ensuring her progress over time remains aligned with her goals. Due to this, Sue found the tool to be a valuable resource for ongoing professional growth and development.

Sue also shared that it would be useful to look back on her Likert Scale for Dual Identities yearly, as she felt this would help to get her back on track for the year ahead. For Sue, annual refection allows for a comprehensive picture of her dual professional identity and progress over the year. Similarly, other FE teachers and trainers shared they would look back every summer holiday, as this is a time they are free from the immediate pressures of teaching or training, and they make clear the importance of choosing a period when they have more time and space to engage in deeper reflection. In this way, FE teachers and trainers might incorporate the Likert Scale for Dual Identities into their yearly reflective practices and existing personal reflection habits. However, Ronnie felt that looking back monthly would make more sense as she feels each month is very different to the next and changes are too regular to make looking back yearly appropriate. For Ronnie, a benefit of reflecting with the tool monthly is that it would allow her to dedicate more time to self-reflection, something she feels FE teachers and trainers should do more often, and to be more aware of her professional identity.

FUTURE PLANNING

Finally, FE teachers and trainers were introduced to using the Likert Scale for Dual Identities for future planning. This stage was described to FE teachers and trainers as one that required them to assess and evaluate their progress towards maintaining or achieving their ideal professional identity. It was outlined that future planning should be SMART (specific, measurable, achievable, realistic, and time based). The extract below outlines Joyce's interaction with this technique.

> I think it's always helpful to think about future planning and I think in this case professional identity is almost like a career path, [the Likert Scale for Dual Identities] is almost like a career coaching tool really.
>
> - Joyce

For Joyce, future planning becomes a crucial aspect of career development and found the tool encouraging, prompting her to plan and work towards her ideal professional identity. The visual nature of the Likert Scale for Dual Identities was deemed highly valuable by Joyce, as it provided her with a clear picture of her professional goals. Joyce found that visualising her goals made them more concrete and attainable and found the future planning stage to be a practical and supportive mechanism for professional growth as it provided guidance, helped her to map out her career trajectories, and assisted her in making informed decisions.

The ease of this stage varied for FE teachers and trainers, and Ronnie found future planning difficult to engage in due to not having a specific goal in mind. However, overall, Ronnie felt that the tool gave her the power to reflect and plan effectively. FE teachers and trainers who have engaged in the tool stated that future planning would help when considering their professional identity and assist them in maintaining or achieving their ideal professional identity, due to its structured approach to monitoring progress. FE teachers and trainers suggested the tool supports their continuous growth and learning and is therefore a dynamic tool for facilitating ongoing professional development.

FE teachers and trainers highlighted the benefits of the Likert Scale for Dual Identities, including its ability to help them maintain focus, provide structure, and foster continuous professional development. Joyce felt the specific nature of the tool was beneficial, as it provided structure to her professional identity and goal setting, while Ronnie comes back to the benefit of being able to see her thought process, which contrasts with the abstract nature of just thinking about her professional development.

CONCLUSION

Overall, the tool was well-received and user-friendly and prompted FE teachers and trainers to reflect on their dual professional identity. FE teacher and trainer engagement in the Likert Scale for Dual Identities has shown it to be useful for those across the sector, from different vocational and technical areas. The tool has shown itself to aid self-reflection on current dual professional identity, ideal professional identity, and future planning. The Likert Scale for Dual Identities has helped the FE teachers and trainers who have engaged with it to understand who they are and why they are; the extract below and Figure 8.1 outline Ronnie's concluding thoughts.

Position: Me								
Ideal Artist	1	2	3	4	X 5	6		Teacher
Dec 2023						X		
Mar 2024					X			

FIGURE 8.1 Ronnie's Likert Scale for Dual Identities.

> Different people bring different things to the table. Someone else would probably be a 3 [on the Likert Scale for Dual Identities] and then you might get someone else who's a 7 and they, in the bigger picture, cancel each other out and make a really good team of people who can educate people really well. I think you maybe need a bit of everyone.
>
> — Ronnie

Ronnie felt that the Likert Scale for Dual Identities increased agency in her professional identity, while Sue felt that it also increased accountability for what you are doing and why you are doing it. Additionally, Joyce felt it was useful for coaching as well as personal reflection.

SECTION 2

Conclusion

Vignette: Side-by-side

My teacher self lived at the institution, on my laptop, and in notebooks. My artist self existed within my art-making process, on my laptop, and in galleries. The physical locations of these identities overlapped. The institution that I was teaching in, was the institution that I studied in years prior and is where I started to solidify my artist identity. At home, my teaching practice and art practice took place at the same desk or in my studio. This meant that both existed side-by-side and neither was ever too far out of reach, and they would often spill over into each other, intentionally and accidentally.

Cairns, A. (2022) Side-by-Side. Unpublished vignette.

This section outlined the concept of dual professional identities in the context of vocational and technical FE teachers and trainers. This section drew inspiration from the work of Daichendt (2009) and his work on dual professional identity continuums and Thornton (2013) and his work on dual identities. Additionally, this section looked at my use of the tool, then named the Artist-Teacher Likert Scale, with artist-teachers in ACL (Cairns, 2023) as well as new case studies of its updated use with technical and vocational FE teachers and trainers: Joyce I-Hui Chen, Ronnie Houselander-Cook, and Sue Chillingworth. This section also provided an opportunity to create your own Likert Scale for Dual Identities to allow you to develop a better understanding of your dual professional identity.

Section 2: 5 key take aways

- Dual identities can be understood as the bringing together of two professional identities to create a new one, and these two identities exist on a continuum with the dual identity forming between the two fields of teacher or trainer identity and vocational or technical identity.
- Dual identities can cause conflict; however, reflecting on your motivations for becoming and continuing to be an FE teacher or trainer may help you sustain your duality.
- The Likert Scale for Dual Identities is a tool to chart current and ideal identities as well as identity ebbs and flows over time.
- The Likert Scale for Dual Identities visually helps us understand dual identity and identity flux.
- The Likert Scale for Dual Identities can be used as a self-reflection tool and as a tool for future planning.

If you did not complete the *Try This!* activities as you read this section, I encourage you to go back and try them now. These activities have been designed to help you consider your professional identity, and engagement in them can form part of your reflective practice.

REFERENCES

Cairns, A. (2023) *Interrogating artist-teacher identity transformation in adult community learning.* Doctoral thesis, Norwich University of the Arts.

Daichendt, G. J. (2009) 'Redefining the artist-teacher', *Journal of Art Education*, 62(5), pp. 33–38. doi: 10.1080/00043125.2009.11519035.

Thornton, A. (2013) *Artist, researcher, teacher: A study of professional identity in art and education.* Chicago: University of Chicago Press.

Conclusion

> **VIGNETTE: SIGNS**
>
> There was a certain mundanity in my epiphany that I was an artist-teacher(-researcher), or at least that I was becoming one. It happened in different spaces, the classroom, my studio, and within my laptop. There were signs, but they were subtle, and it all started with a collection of road signs and a summer spent drawing. As my art practice grew to include signs and symbols, so did my session plans.
>
> Cairns, A. (2022) Signs. Unpublished vignette.

This book has focused on the dual and multifaceted professional identities of vocational and technical FE teachers and trainers in a UK context. Managing your professional identity as an FE teacher or trainer is of high importance, and the two tools presented in this book; networks of enterprises and Likert Scales for Dual Identities are key to helping you in this area. Our FE teacher and trainer identities emerge from our vocational and technical backgrounds, and I hope that this book helps you to find a way to merge these, and other, distinct identities into one professional identity that you are content with embodying. There is a personal significance in comprehending and managing your professional identity as an FE teacher or trainer related to understanding and taking control of who you are and how you operate, but also in understanding how to change your professional identity if needed by planning for and engaging in appropriate CPD activities. Identity is in a state of flux, and we must adapt our FE identities to fit into an ever-changing world. Revisit this book and the two tools presented as your professional identity, or the FE landscape shifts. This book also has wider implications for the FE sector, and as your understanding of your professional identity increases the likelihood of staying in your role may increase, which would positively impact the retention issues within the sector (Mutebi and McAlary, 2021).

THE TOOLS

Within the pages of this book, I presented two professional identity tools designed for handling your complex professional identity: networks of enterprises and

Likert Scales for Dual Identities. To recap, the network of enterprises is a type of diagram first used by Wallace and Gruber with creative people at work (Wallace and Gruber, 1989) to track and chart enterprises over time, with a focus on goal achievement. To create your own network of enterprises, name your multiple enterprises, pick a timeframe to plot your enterprises against, assess the significance of your involvement in each through your selected lens, and consider future planning, including goal setting. The implications of using this tool include a better understanding of the multiple enterprises you engage in and how these impact your professional identity. Additionally, the tool should help you to move towards goal setting in your professional career which will guide you as you plan and engage in appropriate CPD activities.

The Likert Scale for Dual Identities is a tool that draws on Daichendt's (2009) notion that dual identity exists on a continuum and that dual identities come together in the middle of that continuum. To create your own Likert Scale for Dual Identities, name your two professional identities, pick a numerical scale for your Likert scale, pick a colour scheme for your dual identity, place your current and ideal identities on the scale through your selected position, consider your usage of the tool and use the tool for future planning to reach your ideal professional identity. The implications of using this tool include a better appreciation of your dual professional identity, how to change your professional identity over time, and an awareness of how you would ideally like to identify and what CPD activities would aid you in reaching this.

At the end of Chapters 1 and 2 you were encouraged to *Try This!* And develop your own network of enterprises and Likert Scale for Dual Identities, if you have not done so yet *Try This Now!*

REFERENCES

Daichendt, G. J. (2009) 'George Wallis: The original artist-teacher', Teaching Artist Journal, 7(4), pp. 219–226. doi: 10.1080/15411790903158670.

Mutebi, N., and McAlary, P. (2021) 'Upskilling and retraining the adult workforce', POSTnote Number 659, December 2021. Available at: https://post.parliament.uk/research-briefings/post-pn-0659/ (Accessed 17 December 2021).

Wallace, D. B., and Gruber, H. E. (1989) Creative people at work: Twelve cognitive case studies. New York: Oxford University Press.

Index

Note: **Bold** page numbers refer to tables and *italic* page numbers refer to figures.

Adams, J. 19
adult community learning (ACL) 100, 101, 104–105; artist-teachers in 101, 108, 142
artist-educator 34, 36, 41
Artist-Teacher Likert Scale (ATLS) 2, 101, *102*, 104–106, 108–109, 142; dual identity 107–108; real-world applicability of 102; simple tool 110; use 105
assemblages 17, 18, *18*

Barkhuizen, G. 15
Barr, G. 85
Booth-Martin, H. 64–66, 70–71, 73, 75–76, 79
Boucher, J. 13, 64, 72, 77–79
Bourdieu, P. 102
Briggs, A. R. J. 23
Bucura, E. 16, 87

case study tool 38–39
charting experiences 113
Chillingworth, S. 130, 131, 133–136, 138–139, 141–142, 144
colour scheme 116–117, 133–135

communities of practice (CoP) 21–23, 87, 103; multi-membership in 22–23, *23*
continuing professional development (CPD) 3, 113, 128, 144, 145
continuums 101–105; defined 89; dual identity 89–91
creative people 31, 39
Csikszentmihalyi, M. 41
Curtis, B. 13, 64, 73–74

Daichendt, G. J. 2, 30, 34–36, *35*, 39, 41, 51, 55, 83, 101, 104, 142, 145; network of enterprises 37; Wallis' artist and teacher enterprises 38
Deleuze, G. 17, 18
Doncaster, T. 13, 64, 68, 73, 79
Draper, E. 13, 64, 67–68, 76–77, 79
dual professional identity 85–97, 101, 103, 105, 107–108, 118, 134, 137–139, 141–142, 145; continuums 89–91; motivations for 94–97

Education and Training Foundation (ETF) professional standards 3, 24
enterprise audit 45–46, 66

INDEX

enterprise inventory 45, 65–66
enterprise mapping *46*, 46–47, *47*, 66–67
enterprises: assessing significance of involvement 51–57; future planning 57–62; identifying 45–49; naming 44–49; network of 44–62; seeking 48–49, 68; timeframe 49–51; timeline 47, *48*, 67–68

Fairgrieve, A. 13, 64–65, 71, 79
flux 39, 102–103, 107, 144; charting 39
further education (FE) 3–4
further education (FE) teachers identity 2; aim of exploring 4–5; purpose of exploring 4; structure of exploring 5–6
further education (FE) teachers/trainers 1–2; assemblages 17, 18, *18*
assessing the significance of enterprises 70–74; enterprise audit 66; enterprise inventory 65–66; enterprise mapping 66–67; enterprise seeking 68; enterprise timeline 67–68; future planning 75–76; naming your enterprises 65–68; passion lens 73; personal lens 73–74; picking a time frame 69–70; professional lens 74; professional location 23–25; reflections on network of enterprises 64–78; remuneration lens 73; time 72
future planning: enterprises 57–62; FE teacher and trainers 75–76

goal achievement 40
Gruber, H. 1–2, 13, 30–33, 36, 51, 79, 145; creative people 39; network of enterprises 37, 41
Guattari, F. 17, 18

Heathcote, K. E. 13, 64, 66–67, 69–71, 75, 77, 79
hooks, b. 22
Houselander-Cook, R. 130, 132–135, 137–142
Husband, G. 13, 64, 67–70, 72, 75

ideal artist-teacher 101, 104, 105

identities: artist-educator 35; awareness 22; charting experiences 113, **113**; conflict 91–94; continuums 83; dual 86–90, 94–96, 107–108; dual professional 86–92, 97, 101, 103, 105, 107, 108, 118, 134, 137–139, 141–142, 145; FE teacher *see* FE teachers identity; flux 18–19, 22, 83; Likert Scale for Dual Identities 112–114; multifaceted *see* multifaceted identities; pedagogised 21; professional 2, 4, 13, 16–17, 19, 21–26, 32–34, 36, 46–48, 54, 66–77, 79, 86, 102–103
identity conflict 91–94, **94**; overcoming 93–94

Joyce I-Hui Chen 130–138, 140–142

Kong, M. 15

Lifelong Learning UK (LLUK) 24
Likert Scales for Dual Identities 1–2, 4–6, 83, 100–110; analysis of 124–127; case study from published literature 104–108; coloured scale examples 117–118; colour scheme 116–117, 133–135; defined 101; documenting flux 102–103; dual identity 107–108; early use 104–108; FE teacher and trainers' reflections on 130–141; future planning with 127–129, 140–141; identities 112–114; limitations and updates 108–110; naming 131–132; numerical analysis 126, *127*; numerical scale 114–116, 132–133; overview 100; placement 118–120, 135–137; purpose of 101–102; reflection 123–127; static tool 108–109; statistics 105–106; 10-point scale 108; timeframes 120–123, *121*, *123*; usage and averages 120–123, 137–138; use of 101–102, 105, 112–129; visual analysis of 125, *126*

Martin, D. A. 17
McAdams, D. 16–19

148

INDEX

Menter, I. 16
motivations for dual identities 94–97
multifaceted identities 15–25, 37–38

network of enterprises 1, 5, 30–42, 44–62; case study 34–38, *35*; charting flux 39; creating 61; Daichendt's 37; FE teacher and trainers' reflections on 64–78; future planning 57–62; goal achievement 32–33; goal setting 58–59, *59*; goals of 40; Gruber and Wallaces' 37; limitations and updates 38–41; naming of enterprises 40–41; overview 30; revisiting 59–62, *60*; significance of involvement 33–34; use and purpose 31–32
network of enterprises lenses 51–57; passion 53, *53*; personal 53–54, *54*; professional 54, *54*; remuneration 53, *53*; scaling 55–57; time 52–53, *52*
numerical scale 114–116, 132–133

Parker, T. 104–105
placement 118–120, 135–137; factors 119–120; five positions 118–119; prompt questions 120

Plowright, D. 85
professional identity tools 144–145
professional location 23–25

rhizomatic maps 17, 18, *18*
Rutstein-Riley, A. 16

scale anchors 115–116
Schutz, P. A. 16
Steadman, S. 15, 16, 91, 103; *Identity: Keywords in Teacher Education* 16
Storm, J. K. 17

Thornton, A. 83, 101, 116, 128, 142

Wallace, D. B. 1–2, 13, 30–32, 34–35, 38, 41, 51, 79, 145; creative people 39; multifaceted professional identity 37; network of enterprises 37
Wallis, G. 34
Wenger, E. 31, 33, 41

For Product Safety Concerns and Information please contact our EU representative GPSR@taylorandfrancis.com
Taylor & Francis Verlag GmbH, Kaufingerstraße 24, 80331 München, Germany

www.ingramcontent.com/pod-product-compliance
Lightning Source LLC
Chambersburg PA
CBHW061717300426
44115CB00014B/2722